PSEUDOFED'S GUIDE TO TENNIS AND LIFE

From The Number One Tennis Parody on Twitter @PseudoFed

PseudoFed

Copyright © 2015 PseudoFed
All rights reserved.

ISBN: 1514289245
ISBN 13: 9781514289242

All rights reserved. No part of this publication may be reproduced, stored in retrieval system, copied in any form or by any means, electronic, mechanical, photocopying, recording or otherwise transmitted without written permission from the publisher and author. You must not circulate this book in any format.

All characters appearing in this work are sort of fictitious. Any resemblance to real persons is probably coincidental.

Amazing book cover courtesy of the incredible

Mr. Grass and Mr. Alda

Much love to you both My friends

TABLE OF CONTENTS

Personal and Special Thanks		ix
Chapter 1	An Introduction	1
Chapter 2	Tennis	9
Chapter 3	Tennis Rules and Tactics	22
Chapter 4	The Life of a Professional Player	40
Chapter 5	Food and Exercise: A Pre-Introduction to Spirituality	58
Chapter 6	Spirituality	72
Chapter 7	The Ghost Hunt	79
Chapter 8	The Power of Not Now	104
Chapter 9	The Psychology of the Perceptions	120
Chapter 10	Meditation	133
Chapter 11	Guided Meditation	155

Chapter 12	Relaxation Techniques	167
Chapter 13	Dreams	188
Chapter 14	Goodbye	204
Glossary		223

PERSONAL AND SPECIAL THANKS

I would like to take this opportunity to thank some people, in no particular order, without which this book would not have been written.

First and foremost I would like to thank Myself. I have always been there, not only during the great times but I never abandoned Myself in the good times either. Without My actually doing the writing, this book would only have existed in My head and what a shame that would have been for the world. Thank you. I'm welcome.

To special staff member, Del. Thank you for the endless support, friendship and most of all love.

Honorary staff member Julie for the friendship and book editing.

Long time staff member GF for the editing and for being a wonderful GF through the years.

Staff Member Ajda for encouraging and motivating Me to do this sooner rather than later.

Every GOAT has a Chariot and this GOAT is no exception. A very special thank you to Mr. William and his team of Chariot Pushers for the dedication and attentive assistance, especially during wet conditions.

I'd like to also give very special thanks to a couple of sisters:

- The first sister was somebody who had the confidence in supporting Me when I was a little GOAT, unknown to the world. Whenever we see each other she refers to Me as 'gorgeous' (obviously) which makes Me do the blushings.
- The second sister I'd like to thank for constantly making Me laugh so much using multilingual communications when we are both in various parts of the world.

I love you both. Big hugs to all the extended friends, family and pets.

Lastly, as much as it pains Me to say this, without My twitter followers there would not be PseudoFed. I want to thank you all for the support, you are truly amazing and I am so thankful to each and every one of you.

You are all the GOAT.

1

AN INTRODUCTION

Spiritual GOAT Quote:
"To shank, or not to shank, that is the question."

— PF xx

It is not a peculiar feeling when you have the awareness that your very words are and will become history itself, not for Me anyway. Despite being asked to write My book on many occasions by fans, well-wishers, staff and small animals, I have refrained due to My day job which you may have heard about. I am of the full appreciations that having a book written by Me in your small home is something to treasure but please forgive Me and try to understand that I could not rush Myself just to meet the demand until I was ready. I had to choose the correct moment, the right times and moment of PerFection. For the examples, I could have written this book when I was a little child, small in size, and kept it in one of My stylish bags until the right moment to present it to the world. The problem with this method is that, at that time, I was too busy training with My physiotherapist preparing My body for when it was older so it could become a champion, or as we say in Swiss French, champignon.

As this book will be preserved for generations to come and long into the distant future, I will address those people first. Hello future person. My name is Fed, PseudoFed. I am from your past and was commonly referred to as the GOAT (Greatest Of All Time) for reasons which are apparent and obvious as you look back and study My life and career. I imagine you took a syllabus on it at school. I am sorry you were born too late and missed Me, though not as sorry as you are. By now you will know that in My spare time, outside of being a fashion icon, I played a little tennis and was rather good at it, even if commentators said so themselves. If, by the time you read this, you have invented the time machine, please do come back and watch Me play. I recommend visiting the years of around 2004 to 2007. Please avoid 2008, especially the French Open and Wimbledon. Come to think of it, you would probably want to give 2013 a miss too. For the sake of humanity, please take a second trip and travel back further in time too in order to take copies of this book to cheer up the people of the distant past. Just remember and try to imagine the hard times they lived in, they did not have the electricity, running water and worst of all, they did not even know of My existence. I know this will test your empathisations, but it is for the greater good.

Now I will write a brief note to the good people of a very long time ago. Hello. This is a little off topic but do you know a family called the Flintstones? They will become quite famous so do try and ask one of them to autograph a rock for you. Anyway, I can only imagine how difficult life is for you, literally. Despite this, I urge you to try and stay healthy and be strong in the hope that somebody from the future may not only travel back in time and give you this book, but that they come with what is called the modern technology. It may be in the form of little portable screens. Forgive Me, you don't even know what a screen is. It is like one of your stone tablets that you currently use to carve messages to each other, but ours are much lighter and more expensive. I imagine the battery on our tablets do not last anywhere near as long as yours. The person from the future will have one and by looking at it you will be able to see and enjoy My matches of the tennis. Please note this will not be witchcraft, it is merely some advanced gadgetry that you are not clever enough to have.

Actually there are many reasons that suggest that people from the future have already traveled back in time. In Rome (Italy) they built a very big stadium hundreds of years ago called the Colosseum, you may have heard of it. This is direct empirical evidence that they had made the (incorrect) anticipations that I was going to be born much earlier so they wanted to build an arena where as many people as possible could see Me play. I must say they have let the place run down a bit. The facilities are not that good and the players' dressing rooms are virtually non-existent. After all this time there is still no talk of a roof either. In Egypt, many thousands of years ago, they also built large monuments for Me. Although we should bear in mind that this is going back to a time before the Romans. The Egyptians did not have the same technology as the Roman people and at that time they only knew how to build triangular shaped buildings as they were not aware buildings can be round, oval or any shape for that matter. They called them pyramids. All they had to do was trim the sides a little to create some variations. Though to be fair, we could argue that they were more advanced than those that built the Colosseum, at least the pyramids had a roof.

It may surprise you to know that My childhood was rather ordinary. Well, not in the sense as it being the same as yours, I always knew that I was different and would achieve great success. Nonetheless I still had to go to school and do My homework just like you, well, not quite like you. Remember kids, it is important to get a good education and learn things. You need something to fall back on when you aim to achieve what I have and fail. Always do your school work, eat a good breakfast and be polite to your staff. So many people say school times are the best days of your life but I am here to tell you that this is not true. Winning multiple Grand Slams and being the GOAT is far better than double maths first thing on a Monday morning.

It is important for Me to reassure you that I wrote this book Myself with My very own hands and brain (part inside skull). I was offered a ghost writer but I ferociously declined. Apart from wanting to connect with fans personally, I did not cherish being interviewed by a ghost so they could gain information to write this. I think it would be rather scary and I would be making the jittery faces. How do you look them in the eye? How do you know when they have left the room? Can they even hold a pen or type in order to actually write something? More importantly I have watched the serious documentaries called Paranormal Activity and was given the geebeegeebees, but more about ghosts later. No fans, this is Me writing this book and only Me I can assure you with the reassurances. Not a tarot card or pumpkin in sight. Although I quite like pumpkin pie if I may make the honestations.

So what is this great book about? I can almost hear you ask yourself this very question excitedly. Is it just about Me? Well, as much as I know you want Me to say yes, it isn't, well, maybe a little bit. OK, more than a little, actually quite a lot. This great piece of literature is all about Me giving back to humanity and providing vital wisdom and knowledge that is in My possession and being. The knowledge is not separate to Me, I am the knowledge, I am that which is. I am fully of the aware that I have fans from all of the walks of life but we must remember that there are some people that have not heard of Me yet. I know this is a shocking resolutions but it is true. For those unfortunate people, I will introduce tennis itself from the very basics to My personal advanced tactics that I have never disclosed before, not even to Myself, so this will be interesting. Vital information that has taken Me from being a very small baby child to a humble gold sequin cardigan wearing Champion of the World. Once we have covered this subject with the meticulations I will then discuss what it is like actually living life as a professional tennis player. This will explain all the intricacies and faculties of how to prepare for the tennis circuit. Some of you may have the notion that it is all about fast cars, expensive homes, hotels and stylish clothes. That certainly is the majority of it, for Me at least, but there is more that you must know in order for you to be prepared should you choose to take this path.

Then the real purpose of this masterpiece will unfold before your very eyes. I will help you tap into the core of your being, your inner true self. This is commonly referred to as the belly buttons. I will help you achieve your potential, even though it will be far less than Mine.

How will I do this? I will tell you about the psychologies of the brain. You will learn about the cognition and how this affects your life times in every moment. Not just one cognitive faucet, but many. You will learn about perception and why yours is different and inferior to Mine and exactly why this is so. Moving on from this I will introduce you to spirituality and the power of *not* staying in the moment. Spirituality means different things to different people so I will cover this and show you how to grasp the concept (semi-western grip) to take control of your life and make the happy faces. Some people talk about spirits and ghosts when they are referring to spirituality and I will make the big revealings that in My spare times I like to go ghost hunting. It isn't just Me, other tennis players and commentators do this too and we often go together so I will recount one of the most memorable trips. Whether ghosts exist has been a question humans have been asking for a very long time, I hereby will announce the results from our findings so we can finally answer this question and help humanity and raise consciousness to a new level that has never been realised before. In addition, I will explain the other areas of spirituality too, little known things like meditation techniques including a personal guided meditation, from Me to you. I will recount a true story of when Me and Stanford went to Nepal together which was the first time I learned about meditation and enlightenment. As well as this, I will talk about the importance of relaxation and finding 'Me' time so you can learn to love yourself with total acceptance and appreciation. For the first time ever you will see My personal poetry, just one of the many things I do to help Myself relax. Each new theory will be accompanied by a little personal story so you can follow the journey I had and maybe this will help you in yours.

The book will also include a Glossary of some important people in tennis, past and present (not future), that you should look out for. A lot of people tell Me that I am tennis and nobody else matters. Even though this is entirely true, I still like to give the recognitions to other people too, sometimes. Perhaps you can use this and take this book with you to the tennis matches and use this reference section to look up interesting locker room facts about your favourite player other than Me. You will learn about the whole tennis family including the top commentators and journalists, it is all designed to help you enjoy and appreciate the game and ultimately, Me.

Regardless of whether you enjoy tennis or not, join Me on this wonderful journey. You're welcome.

2

TENNIS

Spiritual GOAT Quote:
"When life gives you lemons, ask staff
to make you lemonade."

— PF xx

For those not familiar with tennis, it is a game. It can loosely be likened to the sport of cricket except in tennis a match does not last for days and days, unless Nicolas Mahut and John Isner are playing each other. The dress code in tennis is quite similar to cricket in that one should wear white, especially during Wimbledon. In addition to this, both games involve a form of a bat and a ball. For your important information, in both games, the bat is used to hit the ball. The bat in tennis is called a racquet and has a tight net across its face, but this is not to catch things with, especially fish. Fish belong in water. You may be aware that there is also a net in the game of basketball but it is not very good as it tends to have a hole in the bottom of the basket. It has been like this for years and I am surprised it has not yet been rectified. In tennis the net is part of what makes up the bat that you use to hit the ball back and forth with your opponent. There is also another net on the court itself and the purpose of this is to separate the players and to prevent us fighting during a match. The tennis court is rectangular in shape, which you may be familiar with if you were good at geomography in school, and it is played in an arena where fans come to watch Me play. To make the simplifications, have you heard of the game called table tennis? Well tennis is very similar except that the table is much bigger and you stand on it.

Tennis is played on three surfaces, grass, hard court and unfortunately clay. Sometimes it is also played on carpet, but personally I try to discourage it as I do not think it right and a little dangerous that it is played in the living room. The marks left from the tennis shoes can be a real pain to vacuum out. Grass, apart from being usually green, is the most prestigious surface to play on and by far the most difficult to master. This Grand Slam is of course played in Mr. Wimbledon's large garden and is by invite only sent via telegram, certainly not email. If you win this tournament you know that you are rather good. I have and am. As I mentioned previously, in order to play in this tournament you must wear all white clothes. It is illegal to wear any other colour, if you do you will be arrested and probably spend time doing some form of community service such as working in an office 5 days a week. Some people say that what I do is also a type of community service in that I allow people to watch Me which pleases them. As well as having to wear white at Wimbledon, although this does not extend to undergarments, I personally would always recommend white lingerie for this tournament too in order to prevent the awkward see-through moments. Camera lenses nowadays are much better than they used to be, so one must ensure that the television crew and photographers focus on the balls.

Hard court is where we spend much of the year including two Grand Slams. I'm not sure what it is made of but it is hard. Perhaps it is made of a special scientific material created by very clever people with white coats and small spectacles in the laboratories. This surface tends to be fast in that the ball bounces quickly. I like the hard courts a lot as My legs do not do as much runnings. As one gets more senior in years, energy conservation becomes more important so always make sure that your homes are well insulated for the Wintour.

Clay on the other hand is this filthy dusty material that just gets everywhere. It really is not very civilised and is horrid to stylish clothes. Clay is often orange

PSEUDOFED

but once upon time it was blue and I am, and remain, the undefeated World Champion on this particular surface. For some reason we seem to have a seemingly never ending season of clay that reaches a crescendo in Paris at the French Open. I am not going to criticise Mr. Garros, however, I think he and all the other clay tournament boss people must wake up to the fact that I've always hated clay and they should have switched to a hard court by now.

Let us examine the four Grand Slams with the little details:

To watch tennis at Wimbledon as a spectator one must be dressed with the appropriations. Some sort of evening gown for ladies and a tailored suit for the gentlemen will suffice, perhaps include a pocket-watch to guarantee yourself a good seat. On hot days try and remember to bring a hat, preferably a bowler hat for men and some sort of bonnet for ladies. Always remember the correct protection against the sunshine as the sun is very hot. Some people tell Me that the sun is a star but this is incorrect as stars only come out at night, are very small and twinkle. The sun on the other hand, is yellow, much bigger and goes to bed at night. Mr. Wimbledon has a number of courts available for the little guys (other players) to play on. I only play on Centre Court although insist, on very rare occasions, that I play on Number One court too as little things like this keep Me humble. For refreshments, Mr. Wimbledon's staff lay on a wide variety of food for you. These include, of course, strawberries with the creams and a very traditional fish and chips, just don't ask for the chips on their own as this is not allowed and you may have a point deducted. Chips come with the fish at Wimbledon whether you like it or not. If you are from America, I am making the references to french fries and not the potato chips that are purchased in crinkly and noisy bags. If you are visiting from France or other French speaking countries, like Canada, I am talking about pomme frites. If you are from a Spanish speaking country, I am describing nachos. Despite this, there are also some small options for vegetable people too so all in all you are sure to have a good time. These are *your* choices, Mine are much better. Try to attend the other courts whilst waiting for Me to glide onto Centre Court, it gives the little guys some confidence that they sorely need. You won't need an umbrella to watch Me play as Mr. Wimbledon built a roof for Me which was his pleasure. The ball servants at SW19 are among the best in the business and never give Me cause to make the irritated faces. In addition, the ground staff with their little green uniforms are second to Me.

In the United States of America the Grand Slam is held in a meadow. The facilities there are great and there are lots of them including a food village.

Not a village made of food like cute little gingerbread houses, which is a little disappointing really. Although to be honest it does not really resemble a real village either; there is no Town Hall, no school, parking is terrible and there is no post office. However, having said this there are many food selections, too long for Me to list them all, suffice to say that whatever your taste, you will find it there. My favourite place is the Champagne Lounge which is like homes from homes. Unlike in Wimbledon where Centre Court commentators sit in a very small garden shed, commentators at the U.S. Open have much bigger offices which are situated very high in the sky. The ball servants tend to throw the balls high in the air when passing to each other rather than roll them along the ground, but this is quite pleasant to watch. The ground staff are very polite, smart and always wish Me a nice day. They also say 'You're Welcome' a lot. I'm surprised nobody has briefed them on protocol when meeting Me when they should be saying, 'I'm Welcome'. This is OK, you can't have everything in life. Well, you can, I just choose to accept this as it keeps My little feet on the ground. When it rains at the U.S. Open, they seem to dry the courts with bathroom towels which is interesting and fun to see. I have heard people complain about this, but I think the opposite, it shows a very caring attitude and illustrates how much they love the court. In many ways it reminds Me of being at homes watching staff do the floors.

Down in the under is Melbourne, home of the Australian Open. Quite a remarkable event in many ways, especially that every year in January when the tournament takes place, the weather is always hot and sunny, if you did not know better you would think it was Summer so I cannot imagine what it must be like in August. Everything in Australia is about sun protection, so lots of sun cream and towels filled with ice, preferably cold ice. The facilities there are unique and dazzling, especially for Me. For you they are great too! It is the only place in the world where you can eat spaghetti from a paper bag. I think if anybody tried to do this in Italy they would be placed in the prison, probably sharing a cell with Silvio Berlusconi. Everybody at this event is always so pleased to see Me so I totally recommend you save some money for a long time, come to this event and enjoy Australia and all its great mates. You will not be disappointed.

Very definitely lastly is the French Open. The fans are great because they love Me and I love them too, each and every one of them. They even prefer Me to their own fellow countrymen. Sadly the surface is clay as I mentioned earlier. As you have heard Me say in interviews on many of the occasions, I am not taking anything away from anyone that wins there, but, in My opinion, it is the easiest of the surfaces to play on. The margins are very wide so anybody can dominate here. Just look at the statistics when you have a spare moment

PSEUDOFED

please. So many people have achieved multiple slams at the French, unlike grass and hard court where people tend not to win many times. Actually, you must be very busy so do not check the statistics, trust My word on it. In addition, mathematical people can make statistics show anything nowadays. I have chosen not to win repeatedly at Roland's event because I don't like to be like everybody else, indeed I am not. The Roland Garros complex is a little more compact than SW19 in that there are little ice cream vendors everywhere that, surprisingly, sell ice cream. In addition, there is also a supermarket for you (not Me) in the grounds where you can buy refreshments and saucisson. In order to play or visit there, Mr. Garros demands that you speak French. On the way back homes be sure to pick up a lovely gift for a loved one. I like to buy expensive toilet water as this makes for a lovely surprise.

These are the main venues for the tennis calenders. There are other small training and exhibition competitions called Masters events and Saint David's Cup, but these are quite different types of challenges. For a start in Masters events you only have matches with players that you already know. I used to enjoy the Masters events but not so much now. In Grand Slam tournaments the first week is great as you often get to play people you have never heard of and when you beat them everybody tells you that you will probably win the tournament. The second week is not so exciting from

My perspective as I tend to play people that I recognise, though at least I have every other day off to do other things. Please refrain yourself from researching which player has the most Masters events as I do not believe these statistics are available on the interwebs and if something is available, it is probably inaccurate. Should you really need this information for a school project or something, please send a stamped addressed envelope to: PseudoFed, c/o Mr. Wimbledon, SW19.

For Saint David's Cup it is very different from every other event in the calendar and to be honest, it is really rather strange. You play on behalf of your country rather than yourself. For much of My career I refrained from this event choosing to focus on Me time. I really got put off it the first time I played which left the scars of the psychologies. Nobody told Me that even though it was just Me on My side of the court, I still wouldn't win if I won. How does that make sense? The explanation that was given to Me was that if I won, then Switzerland won, apparently. Switzerland is a country and much like other countries, this means it is a large piece of land. This has nothing to do with tennis. Only human people can play tennis, not pieces of land. I remember walking on court thinking that all the other Swiss players (and Stanford) dressed the same as Me were there to do the supportings. But no, they were somehow part of the team I was representing. What team? If tennis was a team sport the courts would be much bigger to allow the entire team to play at the same time, like soccer or basketball. If all this is not confusing enough already, during the match a rather rude gentleman keeps jumping out from somewhere and has the audacity to try and tell Me what to do. Where is the security? I remember the first time I played, after the third rest break I had some advice of My own to give him. Hence, these are the reasons I did not make the participations of Saint David's Cup very much in the earlier part of My career. At the time of writing, I have revisited the feelings I had and still feel the same, I do not like it. However, for the sake of adding the achievement to My résumé I have started playing in it a little more. One does not always know what the future holds and I must consider what the career will be after tennis so a full résumé is important to send out to potential employers and to take with you to the interviews.

As far as the Grand Slam events go, they have their own terminologies that you ought to become familiar with. Each Slam is played once in every calendar year. If you win every Slam in this calendar year, you are not only very tired, but you will have what is deemed to be called a Grand Slam. This should not be confused with winning a Grand Slam. If you win four Slams in a row but they are not in the same year, this is imaginatively called a Non-Calendar Grand Slam. If you choose to win an Olympic Gold Medal, as well as winning four

Grand Slams in a calendar year, this is called a Golden Grand Slam. Lastly and by no means leastly, if you win three Grand Slams in one calendar year, followed by one the following year, then two the year after that, this is called a Complicated Grand Slam and guess who has one of these? You're welcome.

So let us take the trip down the memory lanes. The first time I saw a tennis match was on the television set. I was mesmerised by the little ball traveling across the court, the movement just seemed so amazing. Something came over Me and I changed My posture from a relaxed sitting position to crouching very low really focusing on the moving ball with laser-like precision. My little bottoms wiggled a little from side to side and when I saw the opportunity, I pounced, flying through the air at the screen. Of course, I landed on my feet, but still tried to attack the ball. When it was apparent that this was a fruitless task I went back to sitting on the edge of the couch and fell asleep.

Throughout My early childhood that moment remained in the thoughts and even though I was so young, I knew it was to be My destiny. Everything I did became somehow related to tennis. During family dinners I used to insist that My chair was placed at the side of the table with a spare and empty chair next to Me with fresh towels. Nobody was allowed to start eating until I said, 'Play'. After a short time My family really embraced this approach and they applauded every time I took a mouthful of food. When this happened I would wait for the clapping to die down before eating again. When we had pasta, if it was not al dente I would raise My arm and insist mother should check for herself. She would often tell Me to shut up and I would obediently finish the meal. Even though this was difficult to accept at the time, I did later learn the value of telling people to shut up Myself. Something I used to do without fail was after the main course and before we had dessert, I'd change My shirt and occasionally even take a bathroom break.

My tennis obsession continued during the school times. Every morning I would eagerly walk to school carrying My bags, perhaps meeting friends along the way making the small conversations. Once we got in the classroom while everybody else brought in a piece of fruit for the teacher, I would proudly place a urine sample in a little plastic cup on their desk. Because of this I was taken to the Head Teacher on several occasions although at the time I did not understand why, to be honest I still do not. Sitting in her office I found it interesting as she sat at her desk, name tag just in front of her. She used to lean forward with her elbows on the table sometimes looking very irritated at seeing Me day after day. In most of the meetings she was quite pleasant but from time to time she would get quite annoyed almost snapping at Me. Even at that time I took something from these experiences and this taught Me how to conduct Myself at press conferences.

I know you probably have a little job or perhaps you are young enough to still be going to school. Cherish each experience as you just never know if the experiences that you are having now, even if they may seem mundane, may very well be the training ground for something great in the future. Although if you want My opinion, this is extremely unlikely.

3

TENNIS RULES AND TACTICS

Spiritual GOAT Quote:
"Always strive to be the best, even
though you never will be."

— PF xx

In terms of rules, tennis is not full of the complications, you just stylishly hit a ball back and forth with your opponent and sometimes it can be quite fun. When you serve, the little ball must not touch the net in the middle of the court that separates you from your opponent otherwise Mr or Mrs Umpire tell you off. The umpire people sit in a high chair and their job is to make sure everybody plays with fairness and nobody tries to do the cheatings. I do not believe the umpires are strapped in, nor am I sure about whether the seats in their cars resemble a car child seat. If they do, I hope they have straps for them as safety should always come first. When it rains at Wimbledon, the Umpires' parents rush out and wheel them in their high chairs out of the way as the super ground staff pull the covers over the grass very quickly.

In terms of the match itself the objective is to hit the ball so that your opponent cannot hit it back. This can be achieved in several ways. The best way is to make a special serve with the quick speed and preferentially using the wide angles. If done correctly you will hardly exert any energy, please remember this little known fact, especially as you get older. Unfortunately, and on the occasions, your opponent will hit the ball back at you. Should this happen and before you start the swing motion to hit the little ball back again, consider whether you have reason to complain. If you think that you do, raise your arm and look at someone with an angry expression. If you are unable to do this you should consider hitting the ball back. Make sure you allow the ball to bounce as it must land within the designated area. If it gets close to the line you may wish to raise your arm, again, to stop play, but this time ask the umpire to call the special referee called Hawkeye. Hawkeye seems to have a good job, he makes all of the important decisions. You do not need a time machine to remember when the umpires used to make these important decisions themselves. Nowadays the umpire people are there to argue with for some in-match stress relief, a little like an executive toy. As well as this, they all carry the little walkie and the talkie. You should take advantage of this knowledge and ask them to radio to your staff to pass on the Chef pre-prepared refreshments during the rest breaks. Yes, the most important person around nowadays other than Me seems to be Hawkeye and you know, for such an important job I have never met him or her. I have tried to meet Hawkeye because I would like My staff to punch him on the nose as I do not often agree with the decisions he makes. Who hired him? Why doesn't he come on the court and make the accountabilities for his decisions? Why is he always right and who decided he should have this job? Why is he never on holiday and how can he be in more than one place at the same time? As you can see, Hawkeye does give Me some minor irritations and this happens quite often, especially if I am a set down.

Before staff lose My temper let us get back to explaining the game. In My ideal world, you do all you can during a match to not start a rally. A rally is when you and your opponent hit the ball back and forth to each other repeatedly. Nobody wants to see this, especially the fans. There is nothing exciting about it. All spectators really want is to see very short points. Preferably like one of My aces. An ace is when you serve and the opponent cannot even reach the ball to return it. This point in tennis will last approximately 0.3 of a second and is totally exhilarating for the fans.

A little tip! As soon as you serve, start running towards the net very quickly. This can cause the opponent to make the scared faces as they think that you are making a charge which will hopefully put them off hitting the ball back to you. To enhance the effect, you may want to make the shoutings or the gruntings as well just after striking the ball. Again, the objective is to make the point be over very quickly to conserve My energy. The alternative is playing long rallies and this turns into a long match. Eventually the legs get tired and you are staring in the face of defeat, or Rafaello, whichever comes sooner. What is the best form of defence? Avoidance. So in an ideal world you should send tournament organisers chocolates, champagne and signed photographs throughout the year in the hope that they give you a favourable draw and you avoid your kryptonite.

The points system in tennis should be improved and updated. A staff member once tried to explain it to Me and I still do not understand to this day (Friday). Suffice to say that when I lose, I feel I should have won, which is an illustration that we definitely need to make some changes to the game. Another example where the sport needs to be updated is in regards to the shankings, as for some reason, this great skill is not recognised. Well actually, it is but for all the wrong reasons. What is a shanking? Well, to make the coincidental faces, I happen to know a thing or two or three, or four, about this. Allow Me to make the explanations. A shanking is when you surprise everyone by making the ball fly in an unexpected trajectory when hitting it and everybody becomes shocked. It is quite a surprise for Me too. The point I am making is that doing this is not easy so there should be some sort of reward system that rewards you with a reward.

There are other people on the court too apart from the umpire and ball servants during a match. These are the lines people and their job is to look very carefully at each line painted on the court to ensure that it stays straight throughout the match. They have eagle eyes and I generally find them quite annoying. I must say that I have not found them to be very talkative either. They are very quiet, you would not even know that they were there except occasionally when they make a very loud shout. It often makes Me jump and the fur on the back of My neck stands on end whilst My survival 'fight or bite' hormones are released.

During a match it is good to pace yourself. You cannot win it with the first point, unfortunately, because of the way the rules are written. I have campaigned against this for some time but nobody else seems to support Me. This is not surprising really as I do not like to mix with the little guys too much anyway, a few of us get together sometimes but more on that later. The little guys go around each other's houses and play on the video game console machines but I have never been invited. I have never wanted to go anyway, I have My own homes. For the tennis match itself just remember not to exert yourself early on, take some little snacks on court to eat during the rest breaks. I like to take fruit, water, some olives and perhaps mushroom vol-au-vent. Take your time and always be humble during play unless things do not go your way. When the match finishes it does not really matter if you are humble or not, the commentators always say you are regardless, which is rather handy.

The other aspect of tennis you should study is technique and movement, this is important for success. Let us discuss technique: start with your feet, foot positioning determines posture and can make the difference between winning and losing. If you forget to move your feet during play you will fall over and risk injury. The other thing to remember is your racquet, you need this on court at all times. How you hold your racquet is something you must get to grips with. There are several options available such as the Western Grip, Semi-Western, Eastern, Continental, Full English and many more. To be honest I just grip it with My fingers and thumb and for Me this works best. Another important tip is to not let go of the racquet.

Now we have the basics, let us discuss the art of hitting the ball. The angle of the face of the racquet influences how the ball behaves on its way back to your opponent. With this you can create topspin, backspin, side-spin, fast-spin, slow-spin, much-spin and no spin. Personally I just tend to hit it without thinking as I like the surprise, this isn't always a good thing. If the ball connects with the edge of the racquet it is called a shankings as I mentioned previously. I have found that I have minimised My shanking stats by changing to a larger racquet. This helps as the edges are further away. You can actually hold the racquet with both hands and this is called two-handed. However, I'm not sure why this is allowed, where will it end? Three hands, four? I have urged the ATP to look at this on several occasions and they are yet to get back to Me.

Movement is the second factor that requires full attention. First of all remember that you must move on the court so refer back to the importance of moving your feet. Failure to move around the court will make it very difficult to hit the ball back no matter how many hands you are holding the racquet with. Try to make your movements graceful and sublime at all times, even if you are two sets down in the first round of a Slam. Remember you are not a sports person, you are an artist and this never stops. When done correctly, even if you lose a match or your career stats are not looking as good as they used to, the commentators can still say that you lost, but you still looked better on court than your opponent. This illustrates how the movement aspect of the game creates a win win situations, even in a lose lose match.

A big part of your game should be your team and staff. They are supposed to make you feel better and often travel with you. You do not have to take them everywhere, but you can if you like. If you are very successful, you may have your own logo design branding and this will be placed on your clothes so if you lose them they can be returned a little like when I was at school. Make sure that your team also wear clothes, especially some of them. You should provide clothes from the same line that have your logo, this is particularly important when it comes to the hats as this is useful during a match so it is easy for you to identify them as they sit huddled in your box. During a match your team do not have time off just because you are on court. They should do the shoutings of encouragement if you feel down. Personally I would not recommend looking at them. In the past, My eyes have searched for signs of reassurance and optimism during a match only to find them eating snacks and playing with their portable telephones. This is not helpful and certainly not what they are paid for. One staff member told Me that they check Twitter as apparently there is a parody account of Me making the funny jokes and court-side tweetings. Another staff member said that they think that this account is operated by someone in My team. I fired them both.

Surprisingly there is more to tennis than what you do on court. Yes, this is correct, there are factors outside of yourself (not related to out of body experiences) that can and often do influence your career. The main ones are sponsors and journalists.

Sponsors like to be friendly, especially to Me. They are keen to provide clothes, under-garments, expensive timepieces, motor cars, chocolates and the occasional beverage. It seems very flattering at first but then you realise that they want something in return like you having to make personal appearances. This involves kidnapping your body and you wake up somewhere else, usually an expensive hotel. I would say that it somewhat resembles the abduction from the little grey alien people that some people speak of, except in the case of a sponsor kidnap you are usually conscious and well Fed. During one of these personal appearances, you have to meet certain people whilst wearing the smiling faces and shake their hand with your hand. Whatever you do, don't tell them that you don't like their product as this can result in the awkward moments. In situations like this it is best to arrange for staff to make your excuses and recommend to the sponsor that they call Stanford instead. I will speak more about sponsors later.

Journalists are very friendly people and come in all forms but they essentially have the same job. Some write their words in the newspapers as well as the interwebs whilst others commentate during the matches. Strictly speaking, I suppose there are differences in these job descriptions but at the end of the day some of them have a special ability to bring Me into the conversation regardless of what they talk about. From My perspective, it was important to command respect from the onset as this set the tone for the rest of My career. You may want to buy some of them lunch on the odd occasions, though I do not recommend that you do this too often so it is appreciated for the unique event that it is. Too much contact can result in the very grave danger that some of them may become too familiar with you. This can result in them asking for sleep-overs at homes, and you don't want that. I do not share My soap-on-a-rope with anybody. Despite all of these potential drawbacks, it is certainly worth the effort to make the friendly faces with them and remember that they work very hard for a very small amount of money.

This sums up basic and advanced rules and techniques of the great game. Study this carefully and you will begin to appreciate what it takes to be Me. Please do not allow yourself to dream of getting close to My achievements as it would be unfair for you but do not let this deter you from making the participations in the beautiful game.

I'm sure other tennis players have their own opinions on what it takes to be great on the court. Of course, their definition of great will always be different to Mine so I can begin by saying that whatever they say is largely irrelevant. What is the difference between Me and them? The secret and hidden ingredient. Every great recipe has a little je ne c'est quoi, that little something that staff cannot quite put their finger on. For the first time in documented history I shall reveal to you My secret. The faces of the poker!

My first trip to Las Vegas I suppose was much the same as anybody else, Prince Harry aside. You arrive in the private jet, local staff greet you, whisk you through the airport carrying your luggage and moisturising creams and before you know it, you are out in the Nevada desert being driven to a top hotel. The first thing you notice is the cloudless skies quickly followed by flashing neon lights in the windows of inappropriate looking stores. I'm not quite sure what these places are but their marketing ideas are certainly innovative. You can rest assured you'll never see anything like it where Mr. Wimbledon lives. My eyes were wide trying to take in all the different things to see along The Strip. I had never imagined such a thing existed! It was exciting and perhaps some people may describe it as a sight for sore eyes but I am fortunate as I do not suffer from allergies. Everything is bigger, more colourful and louder in the Vegas but in a very positive way. The hotel was no different, everything from the checking-in process to the audacious room itself. At the time I had just started in the professional tennis career so was not as famous as I am now.

This is a story I never get tired of telling. Staff will be the first to tell you that every Christmas Eve I make them sit around the fireplace and listen to Me recount this first trip to the Entertainment Capital of the World. Little did I know this trip was to link so closely to tennis and My success.

I was itching to go out and walk along The Strip after settling into the hotel so I skipped out of the foyer singing The Wizard of Oz to Myself, I was so excited. The people here were very jolly and I saw many different types of characters making the happy faces. I wasn't sure where to go first as the options seemed endless yet somehow all exciting. At first I didn't notice how many people were looking at Me, the occasional person pointing. It was early on in My career so whereas nowadays I obviously expect it and like to acknowledge everyone with the little wave, back then it was quite unusual. My first reaction was that there must have been somebody famous walking just behind Me but I checked and did not recognise anybody. No, people were definitely looking at Me.

I stopped outside a casino to have a look inside and when I turned back to continue walking, I noticed a small crowd gathered around Me taking pictures. I was a little unsure what was going on but decided to go with the flow. A nice gentleman broke from the semicircle of crowd encircling Me, rushed over and asked permission to have his photograph taken. I put My arm around him and said Swiss Cheese and everybody clapped. He was absolutely thrilled.

As he stepped back to his friends somebody shouted out, "Sing Jailhouse Rock!" and everybody cheered.

Why was I asked to sing this? I was not sure of the words and to be honest I am not very familiar with all the modern music so I offered to sing something classic that everybody was sure to know, "How about Mamma Mia? It is one of My favourites!" They looked at Me with little perplexed and confused faces. Did they not know it? How could anybody not know this song? Maybe I had traveled further than I thought and I made a mental note to check a map when I got back to the hotel.

Someone shouted back, "How about Viva Las Vegas?".

I raised both My arms in the air as if I had won yet a Grand Slam and cheered, the crowd all joined in too and I said, "Yeah guys, Viva Las Vegas! I love it here too!" There was an awkward silence, as though they were expecting something. Maybe they still wanted Me to sing a song? "How about I sing Bohemian Rhapsody with the high bits too?". They all looked at each other and seemed to lose interest and quickly began to disperse. People usually like it when I sing the Bo-Raps so I must say that I did feel a little of the offentions. I tried to remember that I did not know these people and they did not know Me (yet) so it was their loss. What a strange experience.

Walking further along The Strip I did notice that an awful lot of establishments here seemed to promote the gambling. I remember wondering to Myself how they all stay in business. Why would anybody open another casino when there are so many? If you see five Italian restaurants in the same road, you would hardly open another, unless you are in Italy. Why had not anybody opened up something more useful, like a fashionable scarf store or something similar? Still, as I was here I thought I would try the luck with winning a little something. I walked into the next casino and stopped just inside the door. It was vast, huge and very big. The first thing I did was to buy some chips as I knew this is what you needed to play the games and have the fun times. I remember searching for the little salt sachets but oddly there were none. Looking around there were a lot of the slot machines and further back I noticed lots of tables with small groups of people huddled around. I headed in that direction wondering what to game to play. I overheard the people at the first table were doing something called Craps which made Me feel a little uncomfortable so I quickened My pace and kept walking. The next table was the Blackjacks. I stood there for a moment but was not keen on having to do arithmetic. I looked around and was little annoyed; with so many tables nobody seemed to be playing Snap or Solitaire.

Resigned that nothing really suited Me I just sat at the next table.

The dealer smiled at Me, "Seven Card Stud?"

"You're welcome," I replied, taken aback but not surprised by her forwardness.

Looking around I noticed everybody at the table looking at each other as if they were keeping the big secrets. I was at a poker table. Never having played before I thought I would just see what I could pick up along the way. How hard can it be?

I was immediately asked about My ante but told them My family is none of their business, they were complete strangers to Me and I wasn't going to tell them about any of My Ante's or Uncles. I then saw all the other players put in a chip so I did too. The dealer then started dealing. I was a little nervous. Upon receiving My three cards I, cupped one hand around the two face down cards and lifted the corner to see what it was. I quickly put it down and looked around in case anybody was doing the peepings. The dealer asked Me how I would like to stake and I replied that

I was not really that hungry. I saw the other players put more of their chips in the middle of the table. I noticed one player had the very stern expressions and I could not tell what he was thinking. This interested Me greatly and looked like fun too. It became apparent that this game was not about cards at all but instead trying to guess what your opponents are thinking, a bit like charades but without the party hats. Everybody around the table had similar expressions and on one hand, I liked this as it reminded Me of Bjorn Borg, but on the other hand, I immediately noticed that nobody was thinking outside of the boxes. Before putting My chips in the middle I paused so they all looked at Me; this way I was sure that they would all see My expression. I went to scream just like the lady in the shower in that old movie but even though I was doing the motions, no sound came out. They all look startled. The dealer asked if I was OK to which I composed Myself and said, "yes". Already I knew I had the edge. I threw some chips in the middle. The player next to Me said he would come back later when the clown had left. I looked at all the other players and thought what he said was a little unfair. They all looked fine to Me.

We all received another face-up card each. The dealer stated that the lady furthest away from Me apparently had the best hand so she could bet first. I must admit her hands seemed very well moisturised so I was keen to catch up with her after the game to talk skin regimes. Personally I use coconut oil but it is just too easy to use too much as the smell is just divine. Still, it was very pleasant to note that the person with the smoothest hands was allowed to go first. I remembered giving the backs of My hands a second glance wondering why I had not been chosen.

Everybody looked at each other nervously as each person put more of the little colourful chips in the middle. When it was My turn, with both elbows on the table I leaned forward, squinted so that I could barely see through My groomed eyelashes, and gave every opponent a twelve second glare. The lady with the nice hands said she felt uncomfortable and left which was a big shame. One person remained.

"Are you going to get on with it?" he asked Me quite angrily.

I was a little put out but not perturbed. I just continued to stare at him knowing deep down what this game was really about. After a moment he threw his cards in the middle of the table, stood up quickly and called Me a bad word. I quickly looked at the dealer who rolled her eyes at Me. I am glad she agreed that this sort of behaviour was just unacceptable. Within a few short minutes the student had become the master. This proved that while everybody can get bogged down in any game, the essence is the way your opponent perceives you. I will discuss the psychology of the perception later but for now you can see that even though I had never played this game before, just the feeling of fear I created in those playing against Me was enough for them to lose. Were they better players than Me? Probably, but the point is that I won the game before it even started and as you have seen, this has been the central part throughout My career.

After this interesting and informative experience I went back to My hotel room, finally time to make the relaxings. I called the front desk and asked them to send up several scented candles and a selection of essential oils. As I waited I thought I would slip into the towelling bathrobe and complimentary slippers. Recalling the exciting first day, I looked in the mirror and reflected on My adventures so far. My sideburns seemed a little bushy and longer than I would have hoped. I removed the steel rimmed sunglasses placing them on the table, then I carefully took off the flared white trousers folding them neatly onto the back of a chair. I just could not help but wonder why so many people were staring at Me today.

4

THE LIFE OF A PROFESSIONAL PLAYER

Spiritual GOAT Quote:
"Homes are where the heart is."

— PF xx

The tennis calendar is very long as any professional player will tell you. It is actually much longer than the Gregorian calendar (invented by Greg Rusedski) that you are probably more familiar with. The tennis bosses make us play more tennis matches in a year than there are days. This involves a lot of traveling, hotels and toilets. For Me, in addition to this, I also have to think about the logistications of having staff in every conceivable location in the notice of a moment. This life sure is fun but it is also extremely tiring and is the reason why so many players retire during their late twenties and thirties rather than at sixty five. We do not get any individual holiday leave either, which really is quite unfair. The only times we can have the vacation times is when there are no tournaments or, if you do not reach the latter stages of a tournament, which I occasionally choose to do, not often, but sometimes. So if you play like this and lose a lot, then you have a lot of time off. If you do this more regularly and on a consistent basis, you will not play at all and thus have more time off than you perhaps anticipated when you began your career. Going back to the tennis schedule, I have never quite understood this way of the thinking about allocating leave time. Imagine in your place of work if everybody took time off at the same time and for the rest of the time you are always there. Yes, it sounds inappropriate and inefficient, but it is what we are forced to do in tennis. The end result is that there are probably three or four weeks a year when the poor fans have nothing to watch. What are they supposed to do?

If you do not believe what I am saying try and call the ATP tennis helpline during early December and you will see that your call will not be answered. You will probably hear a recorded message saying that there is an unusually high call volume at the moment and that you are on hold and will be answered in mid-January. It is because of this endless work and metaphysical endurance that I have dedicated a small part of this book to wellbeing as you will go on to read.

PSEUDOFED

The other evening staff and I sat around a rectangular table, Me sitting in the usual position at one end, I made them calculate how many people there are in the world compared to how many professional tennis players there are. You will be surprised to learn that there are more people on the planet that do not play tennis for a living compared, to those that do. I was totally speechless and did not say anything for eleven minutes. It was like one of those moments when you look up into the sky at night, gaze at the little stars while they are making the twinklings and wonder how they stay up and who put them there. The ceiling must be very high, certainly higher than any I have at homes, I think. So even if you do not play tennis, which you probably do not given My recent discovery, you still must look after yourself and your physical body. If you do not, nobody else will. It is different in My case as I have staff to tend to such things.

This aside, let us look at one of the main areas of the professional tennis life. This is the notion of the sponsorships. Sponsors are very important people. Having said this, you will learn that they are not as important as they think they are. Although as a player it is in your interests to allow them to believe that they are very important so please make the note about this. On the other side of the gold coin they really are quite important as they pay you a lot of money and this is quite handy, especially when you do not have any. Present company excluded.

Yes, very early on in your career people will approach you as though they want to be your best friend. They will offer deals that may seem good value such as a free portable telephone or tennis shoes. I have never understood why no sponsor has ever offered some potpourri or lavender bath soap for the homes, it seems so obvious.

Some words of caution must be taken. In the beginning of your career only your family and friends know who you are. Essentially you are alone starting out wanting to make a living in sport. Nobody really knows you because you are nobody, you are nothing. Your influence and power of the negotiatings is close to zero because there are hundreds like you. You are all the same. This is when you are at your most vulnerable. I will offer My early experience of when I met with a sponsor that will no doubt help you during your small and short career.

The first time I was offered a contract was the memorable occasion and adds further weight to the saying that, 'you never forget your first time'. My trophy cabinet was really beginning to get full, it already contained small trinkets and a secret supply of dry roasted cashew nuts hidden behind a photo. Now with the addition of local tournament trophies it was clear that I needed another piece of display furniture. So at that moment I had a little side project and was busy planning an extension to the home. It seems funny now looking back that I only had one place that I called home. It almost sounds as silly as not having your own private aeroplane. But let us not digest, allow Me to go back to the story. At the time I made the extrapolations that at the rate I was winning I needed nine more buildings to house the trophies, for this home any way. I just could not think further than one year at that time in My career. The issue was that despite having the knowing, the inner belief about how great I was going to be, at that time this confidence was not paying the bills let alone outbuildings for the trophies. Can you remember life before I was born? I can't. Yet history suggests that there was life before Me, not a very happy life which is why the dinosaurs died out, but life did exist, somehow.

It was quite early in the morning, I had just finished the breakfast times. This usually consisted of Swiss Muesli, and two slices of toast with butter made from peanuts (crunchy). I find this much more agreeable than butter made from cows. Switzerland is great at many things and muesli is certainly one of them. We make interesting clocks too where little people walk out of small doorways hitting bells with hammers every hour. I do not know what they do in between the hours as I have never seen them come out, goodness knows I have sat there waiting and watching, trying to catch them. Once, I secretly hid a digital camcorder in amongst some comfortable corduroy cushions with the camera pointing right at the clock. When I got home I was so excited to see what had happened to the little clock people. I invited some friends to the house so we could watch the video together that I had made. I had prepared snacks such as popcorn and pasta al forno. When I pressed Play it was totally black on the screen with just the audio of the clock bells chiming every hour. One of My friends asked if I had remembered to take the lens cap off, I changed the subject very quickly and suggested we watch Riverdance.

Anyway, whilst washing the dishes after My breakfast I realised that I was running out of the soap made for plates so made a mental note to buy some more at the supermarket. Even to this day I do not really like making mental notes as I tend to forget where I put them. After cleaning the kitchen and mopping the floor I went upstairs to have a shave, climbing two steps at a time, of course. When I was alone in the house I used to climb the stairs on all fours. Actually this is something I still do today although I try not to do it public places. My bathroom was small but adequate. I looked in the mirror and grabbed the aerosol container that contained the special foam for shaving. This was a new kind that I had never used before. It was a gel, I was more familiar with the foam. I bought it as it was listed as a special offer, with every two cans that you buy you received a mini-travel set including toothbrush and grooming kit. I bought six. I did not think that much of the grooming kit although the exfoliator really did work well, especially on the back of the knees. As I gently pressed down on the nozzle the gel oozed onto My fingers. As I said, normally I would get the regular foam version but apparently this gel turned into foam. I had to see it to do the believings so was very excited.

 After releasing a small portion of the gel onto the left hand I looked at it for a moment. It had not yet turned into foam. I wondered how long I would have to look at it before something happened. When did it know when it had to become foam I wondered. There are so many mysteries in the world and it looked like this was another. With the other hand I tossed the can briefly into the air giving it a slight side spin. It landed perfectly back into My palm with the instructions now facing upwards enabling Me to see them. I gave them a good read and it seemed that I had done what I was supposed to. This was irritating. When would it turn into foam? I should not be expected to wait all of the day times. I had things to do. I decided to try and shave with it regardless. As I applied it to the face something magical happened, it was turning into foam. It knew! It seemed that the circular motions of applying it to the skin caused a reaction of the chemicals and an amazing transformation took place. Gel into foam. It was just fascinating and gave Me the same feeling as when I saw a caterpillar turn into a housefly for the first time. After applying it generously I reached for the razor blade, the best a GOAT can get. As usual, I ran it under the hot water first before starting to shave as I like to warm it a little. There is nothing worse that something cold touching your face. The entire shaving experience was really rather pleasant and the gel left the skin soft, supple and left it with a rather pleasing scent, especially on the forehead.

I checked My look in the mirror and felt quite charmed. The first few bars of Abba's Lay All Your Love On Me chimed on the musical doorbell so I skipped My way down the stairs and to the front door. Who was it at this time of day? The postal service had already been and delivered My monthly edition of a fashion magazine so I knew it was not that. I released the bolt, untied the rope, disabled the alarm with the personal identification number and finally kicked away the novelty rubber cheese-wedge doorstop. I opened the door stepping back slightly as the door came towards Me. A smartly dressed gentleman stood there. I looked at him.

"Hello, Mr. PseudoFed?" he seemed so polite.

"If you're selling household products, please leave as I regularly buy from another agent," I declared. If I am one thing, it is loyal. But I am more than one thing, as by now you are more than aware.

He laughed a little and said he was not selling that. My eyebrows went up with intrigue. "Oh really? You are not selling those plastic containers are you? The ones that you can put things in and freeze, put in the refrigerator or take on a picnic? I have been wanting to get some of those for ages. One of My friends has a set and they are so handy, especially for the leftovers. Do you have any in turquoise?"

Again he chuckled and said he was not here for that either.

That could only mean one thing. "Are you here to convince Me to vote for you? I must tell you now that I do not trust political people too much, they say nice things to get in office and tell you that your life will be nice if you vote for them but when they win they have psychological problems, lose their memory and are the same as whoever was in government before them."

"No, Mr. PseudoFed, I am not a politician I can assure you. I am here because I would like to discuss sponsorship."

Being quite a novice this was a new one I had not heard before. Goodness they try to sell anything nowadays. "Why would I want to sponsor a ship?"

"OK, let me put it another way, I would like to give you lots of money," he finally declared.

This was the kind of salesman I like! I was already hooked. "Do come in, wipe your feet several times and then kindly wash your hands," I said pointing to the small porcelain guest basin beside the front door." He looked startled and surprised although I was not sure why. I watched him carefully and noticed he did not allow the scented liquid soap to froth up so I made him do it again. Once satisfied he turned towards Me and showed Me his hands. I examined carefully and then instructed him to turn them around. He had done well. Once satisfied I pointed at the paper towel dispenser on the wall. I used to have one of those machines that expelled warm air but someone told Me that they spread germs so I had it removed and replaced with the tried and tested method of disposable towels. I led him to the humble living room.

He went to sit down but I pointed to the guest armchair. I sat opposite, crossed My legs and spoke first, "This is not like a real life spam is it? Are you going to say that you have fifty million dollars and that you need My bank details to make the initial deposit? If so you are wasting your time and I will not give you My email account password either."

"No please Mr. PseudoFed, may I call you Pseudo?" he said trying to make the reassurances.

"Yes, you may call Me Pseudo, thank you for doing the askings. I am quite attached to it because it is the name given to Me by My parents, though My birth name is Kal-El. You may use either."

He paused for a moment as though he was taken aback. Not sure why, who does not have a birth name and a parent given name? After a small exchange of the pleasantries he went on to tell Me that his organisation was willing to provide sports clothing for Me whilst I was on tour and in addition pay a considerable about of money into My Post Office savings account. This did not sound right. I am getting clothes and money, surely I should be paying *them*? This is like being paid to shop *and* you get to keep the goods. You have heard of the phraseology, 'If it sounds too good to be true, then it probably is.' This sounded like one of those times.

I asked him lots of questions and it turned out to be true. There were of course some stipulations and when I say some, I mean a lot. I had to wear the clothes provided and this was not negotiable.

"You will become a brand," he explained.

I thought for a moment before answering, "You mean as in the Rock and Roll? You want Me to be like I am from The Rolling Stones with Michael Jagger and Paul McCartney?"

"No, I said brand, not band. Anyway, Paul McCartney was not in The Rolling Stones."

I felt an argument brewing but then realised he was right, "Yes, it was not Paul, I was thinking of Robert Dylan, he was like a Rolling Stone. But what has all this got to do with tennis?"

He looked confused but I was not sure why. I am the one who should have been confused, a moment ago he wanted to get into My savings account and then he starts talking about music. What had all this got to do with Me?

He took a deep breath and smiled, "No, Pseudo, let me explain. You will essentially be representing our organisation, like an ambassador. It is much more than wearing our clothes. Everything you do will potentially affect our image. We will need to discuss your behaviour, especially on court when millions will be watching. Also you will not allowed to wear clothes by our competitors either on or off court."

"It sounds like you want to own Me?"

"Well, I would not want to put it quite like that but, yes."

I looked at the floor, trying to collect the thoughts. I had never experienced anything like this before and was not sure what it would feel like to belong to someone else. Then I remembered that when I was younger we owned a cat so I was trying to see this situation I now found Myself in through the eyes of the little cat we once had.

"How many times a day will I be fed?" I asked curiously?

"What?" he looked surprised at My question.

I continued, "And will it be from tins or those little packets? Will you provide a litter tray and if so how often will it be changed?"

He was the one who was now staring into space before answering. I felt proud of Myself, this was the real first experience of the business side of tennis and I felt that I was already bargaining like a seasoned professional.

He broke the silence, "We can run your twitter account and other social media for you. If you are ever unsure about something you have been asked to do, like perhaps a personal appearance event, either call us or most likely we will send someone along with you to take care of everything."

I was still thinking about what he said about My behaviour, "You mentioned about the way I act on court, can you explain further please?"

"Of course! Well we would not want you to do too much other than play tennis."

Now I was more confused, "What else do you do on court?"

"What I mean to say is, we would not want you to getting into major disagreements with the officials or other players."

"But if the ball is out and they say it was in, you want Me to just accept it?"

"More or less yes, this is what I am saying. I mean, we would not want you to start swearing or anything like that."

I was getting a little annoyed at this point, "Have you ever played any sport before? You do realise that you are full of adrenaline and it could be a major championship. If I see a ball go out, I will say so."

"I understand that, I am just saying we would not want you losing your temper. Just play the game, accept all the decisions and sign autographs at the end of the match."

"Let Me make the clarifications, you are saying that you want Me to be like a robot with no emotion? That makes no sense. Fans want to see personalities. It is what attracts them to any sport and why they come."

"No, you are incorrect and I have a degree in marketing to prove it," he was looking a little tense.

"What about Elvis of the Presleys?" I asked.

"What has Elvis got to do with this?" he said. I am sure that I detected a little anger in his voice.

"When Elvis first started he was moving his hips in the gyratory fashion and this was very controversial. I saw the documentary show on the television set where they used to do the zoomings-in so that the viewers could not see his hips, but everybody knew we was moving them. How many records did he sell?"

"What has this got to do with anything, or even tennis for that matter?"

"OK then what about Johnathon McEnroes? He was a little outspoken and did not like tennis officials being serious. Him and James Connors had some of the greatest matches of all time."

He scoffed, "Yeah and look where that got him!"

"Seven Grand Slam titles, not to mention all of his other achievements and now one of the most respected commentators around. I am sorry, but do you know anything about tennis?" I decided to make My heels dig in.

He looked defiant, "I do not have to know about tennis, or any other sport for that matter. I am fresh out of university and got top marks. In addition I am also the VP for the company, I know what sells."

My heels were firmly in the carpet, "OK I will make the examples, let us assume you are right and you want everybody to act in the same polite manner. But which is more interesting?

Situation A:

> Hello, would you like a cup of tea?
> Oh yes please that would be lovely!

Or

Situation B:

Hello, would like a nice cup of tea?

Tea? Are you kidding me? I hate tea and if you offer it to me one more time you will be wearing it!

What do you think Mr. Sponsor Person, which is more interesting for the fans?"

"I am sorry, but if you want a sponsor you need to accept that things are now different. We are going to pay you a lot of money to represent our organisation and you need to do what we tell you to do."

"I am not sure that I like you," I said.

We both fell silent for a few moments. I actually think that it was longer. I clearly needed the money to help do the advancements of My career and he had the money.

After doing some contemplations I decided that My pride had to take the back seat. I broke the silence, "OK I will do it." Little did he know that I had My toes crossed behind My back.

The rest is history as you very well know. It was the first step of a very long ladder. Though always remember when using ladders that safety must come first, try and get somebody to hold it for you as you climb.

Even though it did not seem momentous at the time, it was an important point in My history. Please study this carefully and do some reflectings of your own, particularly if you want to start out in a sport career. I sincerely hope that the experience that I have shared will assist you. It is too easy to do the arguings on the court, sometimes we must focus not on the steps, but the big picture. It is better to eat humble pie if it means that you have a lovely dessert. And greens too, always eat your greens, kids.

So what is a big picture? How have things changed from then compared to now? Well nowadays when sponsors come to Me they realise that I have achieved the turning of the tables. It is not Me that is doing the desperations for a deal, it is them making the eager and nervous faces to see if I say yes. If I say no, which I do more times than I say yes, then they are very sad, but they have the Little Guys to choose from. Now I can confidently do the pickings and the choosings when it comes to sponsors and they are very welcome.

5

FOOD AND EXERCISE: A PRE-INTRODUCTION TO SPIRITUALITY

Spiritual GOAT Quote. Proverb
Correction Edition:
"There is no time like the present."
Incorrect, there are other times too.

— PF xx

Now I will prepare you for the great wisdom. It will change your life forever regardless of how little you have probably achieved. Let us make the observations, you are not as successful as Me and nor will you ever be, so there is always more to learn. And it is My pleasure to do the sharings. Those familiar with My tweetings account know that on rare occasions I share Spiritual GOAT Quotes. As you have seen, I have included some in this book for your enjoyment and personal growth.

Let us ask the great question: What *is* spirituality? Do you know the answer? Well an actual definition does not exist so if you thought you did know the answer, it would not be very spiritual. With My help I will guide you through this next important phase of your lifetimes.

I am going to start with the very basic level of spirituality, hence this being a pre-introduction, and at this level we shall explore health. For good health you need food. Without this you become a spirit in which case you do not need any food. We need to think about food every day to put in the tummy places. Contrary to popular belief food does not grow on trees so we need to obtain it from other sources. Fortunately, this is what Chef is for. A popular mistake is to give Chef a list each week of the meals you require. This involves an awful lot of time and to be Frank when you have a full time job, it is not a very efficient use of your week. Actually, whether you are Frank or not, the same applies. Chef knows that I need food and he also knows what I like so really this is all and the only planning we both need.

What food should you eat? When should you eat? How much should you eat? Do you need to lose or gain some of the weight? These are a lot of questions I know. I don't know the answer to any of them. I am not a Doctor nor a scientist, nor a geologist for that matter. I use uncommon sense to guide Me and you will agree it has done Me rather well so far. You only possess common sense but do not feel down, this is acceptable and what you should expect. Obviously I am the opposite of common so would be horrified if my sense was anything other than uncommon.

You should eat the breakfast, but only if you feel the hunger. Your body knows when it is hungry and it will tell you via a special feeling in your abdomens. Do not get caught in the trap of repeating phrases and believing them to be true just because most people say them over and over again. For instance, 'breakfast is the most important meal of the day'. If it is My birthday, the evening banquet is the most important meal of the day, not breakfast. Really though, you need meals and none are more important over another but the rule of thumbs here is that you should only eat when you are making the hungry faces.

In tennis you change your eating regime depending if you are playing a match or not, or in the case of facing Rafaello, being played. The last thing you need is to go on court having just been Fed a large meal. You want to eat something that makes the quick digestibles. I would suggest a little fruit and not much else.

Many athletes say you need to 'carb up', perhaps the night before, by eating lots of the spaghetti noodles. Well, not everybody has access to an Italian person the night before a match to cook for them, though I expect Fognini does. Either way I disagree with this statement about doing the carbing up. The last thing I want is My intestines full of big lumps of chewed pasta as I am running around on court. This would not end up with a good result.

After a match you should not eat straight away, allow the body to recover. You could not eat anyway as you have the sponsor and media commitments. I must do the admissions and state that it gets to Me sometimes. You do not even have time for a long soak with bath salts, candles and some relaxing music. A trainer once tried to put Me in an ice bath to speed up the recovery process, he did not make that mistake twice. Immediately walking off court you have to make the quick shower then rush to be interrogated by the journalist people. I do find this one of the most unpleasant aspects of the beautiful game. Who else is forced to essentially go back to work after bathing and still delicately wrapped in their silk robe? My hair is usually still wet, maybe one of My eyes is a little pink from getting the generic ATP shampoo in it as I had to rush only to have to answer something like, "Why did you lose today?" You always know when I get annoyed in these Press Conferences as I give the short answers and make the stroppy faces. Then as soon as I finish I have to do it all over again in other languages such as, Swiss-German, Swiss-English, Swiss-Spanish and Swiss-Cheese.

Anyway, let us return to the importance of the food, allow Me to show you two menus. The first is on a typical match day, the second is when I am not in a tournament and just relaxing at homes.

Match Day (evening match):
Breakfast: Yes. Quite late at around 10:30am. I like to call this Bruncheon. A little muesli with wild picked berries, slow roasted pecans and freshly made almond milk. To drink, I like juices from the orange. No wine.

Lunch: Yes. Around 3pm. Some lightly steamed vegetables, a little fried rice with soy sauce, two dim sum and a free calendar.

An hour later as it is match day, I power up with a green smoothie. I have tried other colours but they either leave Me with a frothy moustache, or even worse as with a blueberry smoothie, make My teeth a funky colour.

Nothing else until after the match but even then only something light before going to bed otherwise I will have bad dreams resulting in having to wake up staff. Not that I mind, it just makes them useless the following day.

Ordinary Day at Homes (no match):
Breakfast: Yes. Around 8am or 6.05am if visiting Boris Becker. Two chocolate eclairs, a fizzy drink and ice cream with sprinkles.

Mid-morning snack: Yes. Time variable depending when the eclairs have gone down. Peanut butter, chocolate spread and sliced banana sandwich in a freshly baked baguette.

Lunch: Yes. 12.05pm As an appetiser, 4 Papadoms with a selection of dips such as: Mango Chutney, Lime Pickle and Onion Salad.

For a starter: 2 Onion Bhajis and 1 Vegetable Samosa

Main course: Mixed Vegetable Korma with Mushroom Rice, Garlic Naan and Aloo Gobi.

Dessert: Warm Apple Pie and Chocolate Ice Cream.

Evening Meal: Yes. 6:30pm or 10:45pm if in Spain.

Baked beans on toast (wholegrain). Cup of Tea and four chocolate cookies, sometimes five.

Please feel free to use this as a guideline and in time you will develop your own regime.

Now let us look at the different types of food we have available as a species. For the examples, you can get salted peanuts, dry roasted peanuts, Jamaican peanuts which are very some-moreish and monkey peanuts. The latter are given that name because they are in their shells which look like monkeys. Although personally I think they look more like the shape of a kidney, but they can not be called kidney nuts because we already have kidney beans and the kidneys would get confused. Already you are beginning to build a picture of the different kinds of foods you can eat. As a tennis sports-person, do not worry about this too much, as the saying goes, 'Why have a chef and bark yourself?'

It is important to have the knowledge of food storage because sometimes you could be playing in a country you are not very familiar with and do not want to eat the food provided by the local tournament organisers so you will need to carry a packed lunch prepared by staff that morning. You could use the little plastic airtight boxes to transport snacks in although do make sure that these containers are BPA free. BPA stands for Be Prepared Always, please do the Googlings for more information on BPA free plastic. If you need longer food storage there is of course tinned food. But such things are much more difficult to open on court and are not re-usable, plus eating a lot of beans during a match can be awkward, especially with today's sensitive boom microphones that seem to pick up everything. Having said that, tinned food is not all bad. If you are sick but brave enough to play a match it can be quite comforting to tuck into some Cream of the Mushroom soup after the first set. Remember to always ensure staff dispose of food waste and containers responsibly.

Different cultures have their own customs and it is good to be aware of these before attending so not to cause the offentions. In Spain it is illegal to have plates so everybody eats from little dishes that are approximately two centimetres in the diameter called tapas dishes. If you are caught eating from a plate you will be made to have dinner at around 6pm rather than the usual 10.45pm. In France you can eat anything providing it is Michelin star French food or you will face prison. A word of advice, do not confuse Michelin stars with review stars given on Amazon or you may end up with a DVD player rather than a Crêpe Suzette. In Italy you can only eat at Nonna's house. You must eat everything put in front of you and promise Mamma that you will put more weight on soon. In China, you will not quite know what you are eating other than there will be a strong possibility that it was alive two minutes before. In Great Britain you can enjoy fine local cuisines like curry and kebabs that are only to be consumed late at night after attending a Public House, or in My case, a Private one.

This gives you a priceless insight from My travels and experience as a champion and ambassador. Please feel free to use this section much like a guide book if you can ever afford to travel.

Keeping your body supple, nimble and looking great is important not just as an athlete, but in your life too. Some people think that playing tennis alone is great exercise. They are correct, though you need to train before you can do this otherwise you will be unable to keep up and you will be doing puffings after a few points. Preparing for this is not just about jogging with your music player strapped to your staff member's arm. As the nice lady from Fame once said, "You've got big dreams. You want fame. Well, fame costs. And right here is where you start paying: in sweat." She was correct in most assumptions although I would disagree, at least for tennis. It does not really cost anything other than a racquet and you can buy these at a very reasonable cost at a local sports store. One of My favourite places is Mr Bradlings' Tennis Nation store in California. He did not pay Me to say this, although he should have. It is not too late Mr. Bradlings.

Having a Personal Trainer is great for the motivations although never forget that they are just another member of staff, make sure they never forget it too. You should always start every training session with some light stretching, especially your cooked hamstrings. I suggest standing on one leg, with the foot of your other leg up on the backrest of a chair and your hands on your hips. Breathe in gently through your toes and exhale through your head, this aides circulation and allows air to flow freely. Maintaining your hands in the same position, lean forward with your chest towards the leg that is propped up on the chair. It may feel a little tight on the back of your upper leg quite high near the bottoms, so do this with care and attention. You need to do this with both legs though, remember to put one leg down before putting the other one up. If you do not feel very stable doing this standing up, you may sit on the floor with your legs straight out in front of you, it does not work if they are stretched out behind you. Again, gently lean forward, preferentially with your arms and hands pointing towards your toes. Do this every day and after several years you may feel a tremendous difference.

Another technique I recommend is strength training. This one is especially fun as you can do this on a beach, preferably your own. You will want to work up to running along the water's edge in the damp sand pulling several car tyres that are attached to your back. This will really build the thigh muscles, back and abdomen. At first start gently by walking rather than running, and begin by pulling a small member of staff. In the unlikely event that you can not find a beach, remember that they are usually situated by the sea. Remember safety at all times so use sun protection on the skin (the part of you under the clothes) and wear a hat. It is nice after such a beach workout to have a cooling ice cream and perhaps a refreshing drink too. If you see anybody offering to take you for a ride along the shore on the back of a donkey kindly remind them that this is not what little donkeys are for and offer to buy the donkey from them to be re-homed in an appropriate sanctuary.

In terms of preparing for a match you should always look at endurance training. If you are facing Rafaello Nadal on clay, I suggest you do not do any training at all and instead enjoy a few glasses of Jägermeister as this will help with the pain and suffering. However, if you have been well behaved all year, you may be lucky and have a draw where he is on the other side. In such a case you can prepare in several ways. The most obvious is the treadmill. This is a special machine with a conveyor-type belt that moves and you run on it. It is an odd sensation because you are running and actually not getting anywhere, I seem to recall a few matches like that. If you do not have a treadmill you can go to a gym or even run outside. You could try running indoors too but I doubt your house is as large as My homes so I recommend the outdoors. Ideally stick to a public park and run circuits. If you have a tournament that is located in a built-up area with no such facilities, then use the pavement or as My American friends say, side-walk. If you are forced to take this option remember to look fashionable whilst dressing appropriately. I suggest some stylish leg warmers, jogging pants and a loose t-shirt. You may want to consider colourful band-aids across the nipples to prevent chafing. If the weather is a little cold perhaps wrap a lovely scarf around the neck area (part under head) and wear a light jacket. Your hair may get out of place so consider tying it in a pony-tail or, My favourite, platting it on each side. This is a great idea anyway if you go out without having showered as nobody can tell if you have washed your hair yet. When returning from such a session try and sneak in and grab a shower before anybody notices. You will be hot, sweaty, quite sexy but probably will not be looking your best so freshening yourself up followed by a quick blow dry and application of body moisturiser such as a little shea butter, it really works wonders.

After any physical session it is always pleasant to take time to relax and have some Me time. Sit in your favourite chair, ask staff to put your feet up and listen to some relaxing music whilst sipping on chamomile tea. It is OK to close your eyes, do not feel bad if you fall asleep for a well deserved power naps. I do recommend a power nap over a micro-sleep because the latter is very small. The only danger during these moments is somebody waking you up with a start, such as a slamming door or a staff member dropping something in the kitchen. There is nothing worse than being woken up confused and startled wondering where you are, eyes searching for comfort and reassurance. You really do not want to wake up like this so do make the precautions to ensure everybody knows you must not be disturbed or there will be employment consequences.

There you have it My fans. Another priceless collection of expert advice helping you grow towards your potentials. From this you will be able to knowledgeably and confidentially source your food, discover what you like but also try new and exciting flavours to tickle your taste-buddies. By studying this guide you will now have an excellent understanding of time management. Advising your chef to prepare only your chosen dishes is a must, as is learning a little cultural background on what to expect when traveling to certain destinations around the planets. One of My favourite perks of this job is being able to travel and meet wonderful people from all over the world. Yes it is great for Me but most of all it is wonderful for them and their lives, it gives them purpose and hope. Once you have mastered how to treat your body on the inside, you can then focus on the outside with the amazing collection of training regimes I have just provided, catering for your every need regardless of whether you are an aspiring player or a fan. Either way if you use these tips, you win in life. Not only is it true what they say about your body being a temple, it is also the place where you live.

6

SPIRITUALITY

Spiritual GOAT Quote:
"When in Rome, you are in Rome, that
is the question."

— PF xx

You now have the ultimate knowledge of tennis, expert techniques and tactics that I have never revealed before. In addition, I have also talked about health, diet and the exercise. This in itself is worth My weight in gold. Is this enough? 'More than enough GOAT', I hear you cry. Yet I choose not to stop writing for you, as tempting as it is for Me to do so. Now we are almost getting to the core of My message, the knowledge that will enable even you to achieve a little more in your life. That chapter exists to discuss spirituality. What is spirituality? Some people consider it relating to the New Age, but I think you can do this at any age. You can do this half-way through the year or when you reach a new age, often referred to as the Birthday. Other people think that it is something to do with tree hugging. I am actually a big fan of hugging and think we should all exchange cuddles and often. You will notice us tennis players always have a hug at the end of each match. Sometimes it is somewhat difficult to do this if you have had the little argument during the match itself but still, it is important to ensure that you put the differences to one side in order for the hug to take place. These differences can always be brought back later or indeed the next match, often referred to as a, 'grunge match'. I know that I speak for all the other players when I say that we also would like to give the Umpire a hug when the game is over but they insist on sitting in the high chair often expressing that it is their chair and nobody can make them come down unless they want to, so we have to shake their hands instead.

Never forget to hug yourself too. You may have heard some gurus state that it is important to love yourself. Do not dismiss this as a mumbo jumbo jet. I hereby give you permission to accept this notion with My approval. Do I love Myself? Sure, I give Myself a big hug every morning and at the night times as I am preparing for bed. I often include the self high-five too on the occasions. For those of you that remain cynical, remember that unless you fully accept who you are, you will never be able to enjoy everybody else's differences. Again, some people say that it would be boring if we were all the same and this is something I actually disagree with. When I hear this statement I am eager to engage in the conversations. Surely the first rebuttal to this point is that it depends on who we choose to be the same as. Let us pick somebody at random, you choose somebody right now as you are reading this and so shall I. I will not tell you who I have thought of before you are ready. Ready? Are you sure? Then continue to read on. Yes that is right, Me too! Is it not incredible that we both chose Me? If everybody in the world was like Me we would all be playing tennis and technically we would all be numero uno! There would be no poverty in the world, we would all have homes and there would be no left-handers playing tennis. Does this not seem a dream to you? It is a dream I have rather frequently. Every night actually if I were to make the honestations.

Some people say that we are already all the same, they say that together we are as one. Staff and I think this is a profound point. We all have teeth, apart from little human babies and slugs. Slugs do not have teeth, even as adults, which makes Me do the concernings, does this mean that little slug dentists are all unemployed? Anyway, as I was saying, we all have a heart and we all want to be loved do we not? This is regardless of your religion, culture or number of Grand Slams achieved in your career (not as many as Me). Yes I really do agree with Me, we are the same and have the same needs and I urge you to make the considerations concerning our similarities.

A spiritual Master will tell you that it is the ego that tries to convince us of separation. We all have the ego and it would be foolish to suggest that somebody has not. I certainly have. We need to make the acceptance of this. But the ego is not who you are, it is just part of the brain (the bit inside the skull) and we should question our attachment to this little voice in your head. The fact that you can listen to this constant narrator in your head, incessantly talking is proof that it is not you. Can you shut it up? Not unless you try the meditations, but we will discuss this later. The point staff are making on My behalf is that if this talker in your head is something *you* are listening to, then who is the creator of the thoughts? Who is the listener? You cannot be making the thoughts and listening to them at the same time otherwise why are you bothering to listen? If it was *you* that created these thoughts, surely you would already know what you have created before they have manifested, in which case, there would be no point in listening to what was being said because you would already know what was about to be said? You do not make a lovely sandwich with avocado, sliced tomato, and a little seasoning then act all surprised when it is ready to eat as though it had just appeared and you have never seen it before. You knew you were making the sandwich otherwise you would not have known what to put in it. But thoughts in your head are not like this. You can not eat them for a start. They just appear in your brain, talking, chatting and there is nothing you can do to shut them up, just like one or two commentators I know though I will not mention the names. Unlike commentators, at least you can choose the direction of your thoughts but this is the only control you have. So you see, these thoughts cannot be *you*, because *you* are listening to the thoughts, whilst eating a scrumptious sandwich.

I have also introduced you here to the concept of attachment. I do not mean this in the sense of using glue to stick things together with or when using a hammer with the nails like when a Carpenter begins to make a wooden chair and declares that We've Only just Begun. No, I mean this with the reference to the psychologicals. Allow Me to explain. My fans have an attachment to Me. If you do not have any attachment to Me, put this book down now and give it to somebody that does. When I choose to lose the fans get upset because of their attachment to Me. Somebody sitting next to them who may have never heard of Me, perhaps someone from another dimension, will still enjoy the same match but when they see Me lose they will not be upset because they have no attachment to Me. This is why some people tell you to 'let it go' when you are angry or upset about something, they are referring to the attachment. Attachments can be good as they allow the enjoyments but as you can see, they can make you very upset. When this happens it is the time to recognise the attachment and let go just like those people tell you. After all, while you are upset about Me choosing to lose, I am sitting comfortably on Fed Force One snacking on an ample selection of hors d'oeuvres. I am not as upset as you, does this mean I have no attachment to Myself? No, maybe I am happier with Myself than you are with yourself. Also and perhaps more poignantly, I have no attachment to you, I do not even know who you are. Please do not be offended, I am merely stating fact. If you need further clarifications on understanding the theory of attachment, please watch any televised commentary of a tennis match. Regardless of who is playing, the probability of the commentators mentioning My name is rather large because of their attachment to Me.

Attachment also comes hidden and disguised appearing to be in the positive form but for Me, there is nothing positive about it. At the time of writing, I am choosing to win less matches than I did compared to when I was in the best part of My career. Because of this, some journalists use their attachment to Me to caringly suggest that I should retire. It is so kind of these people to suggest career decisions for Me, especially those that if I have ever spoken to them at all, it is only in the press conferences. Yes, I would like to take this opportunity to thank these characters sincerely and I shall reciprocate by proposing that maybe it is time for them to retire too.

Before we can begin to appreciate spirituality, we need to understand what it is not. I can confirm that it is not anything related to spirits and by this I mean high alcoholic beverages. A little tipples occasionally and in moderation is perhaps OK. It certainly helps Me to make the giggling faces when I do, but remember it is not good for the healthy times and generally speaking should be avoided. It has nothing to do with spirituality and certainly nothing to do with winning tennis matches, let alone doing so gracefully.

7

THE GHOST HUNT

> Spiritual GOAT Quote. Proverb
> Correction Edition:
> "The pen is mightier than the sword."
> Incorrect, pens are very small whereas
> swords are very big and sharp.
>
> — PF xx

Spirituality has several branches, a lot like a tree though to My knowledge, spirituality does not have leaves, nor little birds sitting on it. The main differences between the two are that trees are made of farmhouse tables, chairs and rustic cabins whereas spirituality is not. One of the most important branches of spirituality is that of ghosts. This is true My fans. Lesser gurus than I do not talk about this aspect. They talk about self awareness and things, but I make the encapsulations of everything. Spirituality must also include the things that go bumpy in the night.

Do you believe in the poltergeists and other fearful things that make the creaky door noises in the big old homes with the creaky floor boards? I can tell you right now that they do exist. I have seen them Myself and so have staff. Here I will show you the proofings.

How does one go in search of the ghosts? Can you just ask staff to turn off the lights and then walk around old houses listening for noises from the past and listen out for screaming sounds? Yes, that is one way. But before you do there are some things you need to know. Firstly, there are several types of ghosts and we need to make the awareness of them. Nextly, there is the standard ghost. They normally have a sheet over them with little holes cut out for the eyes. They are very common around Halloween time, at least, this is when I see them. For some reason they are not very tall and when they knock on My door at homes in the evening they always seem hungry. There are also ghosts that make the residual hauntings. This is when ghosts keep replaying a scene from the past over and over again. It is a lot like repeatedly watching that DVD Mr. Wimbledon published of the 2008 final between Rafaello and Me; no matter how hard I try I cannot change the ending, it just keeps playing over and over again. Although experiencing a residual haunting can seem scary at first, especially if this is your first contact with these types of transparent people, please remember that they cannot harm you, in fact, they do not even know you are there as they keep replaying the scene. I do not know about you but when people ignore Me I make the irritated faces as I find it very offensive. Another type of ghost is the poltergeist, though nobody has ever told Me why they are poltergeists rather than polterghosts; this ghost is very naughty and throws your expensive ornaments around the homes. If only it was as easy as sending them to their room, but this would be a waste of times as they could just walk out through the walls. As well as these types of hauntings, we also have another type and this is called the possessions; this is when the spirit takes control of a living person and there is an extreme change in personalities. A lot like the difference in a politician before they get elected and then afterwards when they are in office. Sometimes a special priest can help but for a politician this is not possible as the condition is usually irreversible.

To help with the ghost hunt you may wish to take some equipment with you. Make sure to dress warmly as it is usually quite chilly at the night times. Maybe a hat and some thermal under-garments. I usually also take a flask of organic hot chocolate with almond milk and some snacks for when the tummy makes the rumbling noises. I encourage you to use the technology gadget devices too. A thermal camera, surprisingly, does not keep you warm but instead displays different temperatures of the environment. This enables you to use your eyes (front of head) in conjunction with the device to notice any ambient changes as it is said that a ghost person will draw on surrounding energy, such as heat, and create a cold spot. Without this you would not be sure if the area is an isolated cold spot or whether it is an insubordinate staff member that left a window open (usually the case). The last piece of equipment I recommend is an EMF meter. EMF stands for Electric Magnificent Fed. This measures electrical energy such as the aura emanating from true greats.

Now we have covered the basics of ghost hunting I will reveal a private side of the tennis family. Every year after Wimbledon finishes a few of us like to take a tour of the Wimbledon grounds after the final, very late in the night times or rather very early during hours of the morning when everybody has gone home and is asleep. This secret tradition of the tour has been carried out for many years and although private, I thought it would be nice to share with you. I will recount the ghost hunt of July 7, 2013 after the championships were over. Joining Me was Mr. Bradlings, H.R.H Prince Charles, Tomas Berdych and, unfortunately, Andrew of the Murrays (please see Glossary for details as to who these people are as you may not know them, especially the last one). I had a couple of staff members with Me as well for miscellaneous reasons. We did invite Maria Sharapova but she said she was too busy and sent over a big box of candy. Somebody (not Me) wanted to invite Rafaello Nadal too, but apparently he is a little scared of the dark which I did not know about. Why didn't anybody tell Me before? If I knew this I would have ensured we play our matches at 2am with the lights off.

Prince Charles does not normally attend the tennis matches as he is very busy talking with his plants and making comments on the awful architecture of some new buildings. However, having lived in old homes all his life he appreciates a good ghost hunt.

That night we had to wait for Andrew of the Murrays because apparently he had been out for an evening meal in London with Marion Bartoli. I did not even know they were friends. I am a little fussy with time-keeping, unlike some people I know, so was already agitated when Andrew arrived. Mr. Bradlings announced that one of the most haunted locations in the Great Britain was the Tower of London which was originally built in 1078 and is now home to the Crown Jewels. I told him that they do not house My jewels there.

Before we started Prince Charles suggested we sing the British National Anthem. When we finished Tomas wanted to sing Wham's Greatest Hits but I had to make the interventions and say no, but suggested maybe later on the Twitter.

I noticed Andrew was carrying something, "What is that Andrew?"

"It's the Wimbledon Trophy I won earlier today," he replied with that annoying grin he occasionally does at Me.

"Why is it rattling?" I asked with the curious faces.

"I put My Olympic gold medal in it," the grin now turning into a definite smirk.

I remembered Andrew had a hotel in Scotland and asked, "I'd like to come and stay at the hotel."

Andrew took out his portable telephone, swiped on it several times and said that they were fully booked.

"I haven't told you when I was planning on coming!" I said with the stern faces.

He looked at Me and asked what dates I had in mind and I said either December or in the Summer after Wimbledon, next year. Looking at his phone again briefly he immediately said that they were fully booked for those dates as well. I was certain he was trying to hide that smirk.

"Well, I could buy My own hotel in Scotland if I wanted to, I could even buy two" I said smugly.

He shrugged his shoulders, "So? Why don't you then?"

I looked away.

Prince Charles shook Andrew's hand and told him that he was so pleased that One was Wimbledon Champion. I thought for a moment wondering what he meant. Juan? He did not win Wimbledon. Then I realised that because Mr. Charles probably does not watch much tennis he probably thought Andrew was Juan Martin, it is an easy mistake to make on account of the accent. I decided not to say anything, it was not My business.

After a few minutes of us waiting and staff twiddling My thumbs, Mr. Bradlings asked Prince Charles, "Have you finished yet, Dude?"

"Dude?" Mr. Charles replied sternly, "We are in Great Britain, Land of Hope and Glory and One is definitely not a Dude thank you very much. And whilst I am on the subject, colour has a 'u' in it."

"Hey chill man, I'm just saying can we get going?" said Mr. Bradlings laughing.

Eventually we set off into a very dark Centre Court complex. It feels very different during the night times. No bustle and hustle of all the fans excited to catch a brief glimpse of Me. It feels cold, dark and spooky. It was pitch black which meant you could not see anything. Now I understand why everybody else had hats with the little torches strapped onto their forehead. I nearly asked where they bought these gadgets from as I was quite keen to make the purchasings Myself and they looked very fashionable. I wished I had asked now as it would have been useful to see where I was going. All around us just felt empty, the only sound was that of our footsteps echoing along the walls and ceilings.

Andrew broke the silence, "You don't really believe in ghosts do you, Pseudo?"

"No, of course I do not, Andrew," I said.

But really, I am not so sure. Our human history is filled with stories of spirits, pumpkins and witches that fly on the brooms. I have not studied animal history so do not know if their history is similar to that of humans.

"It's so awesome being here at night with you guys," chirped Mr. Bradlings, "I have a feeling we may see something. You know the latest study said that 61% of people had never seen a ghost meaning 39% had or weren't sure, that's quite high."

I was trying very hard to listen over Mr. Bradlings' incessant discussion on statistics. Seriously, is there anything he does not know? I thought it was just sports but he seems to know every number on every subject.

Suddenly I heard a shuffling ahead of us, "Did anybody else hear that?"

"No, One didn't hear anything," said Prince Charles. Why was he speaking on behalf of Del Potro?

"Actually, I thought I did hear something," agreed Andrew.

"Did One? Perhaps One did too," said the Prince.

I couldn't take any more of it, "Look, Juan is not here!" I said making the exclamations.

Mr. Charles looked at Me making the bemused faces and said, "Well One certainly looks here to me, I'm looking at One as I speak."

"I do not look anything like Juan!" I snapped.

Mr. Bradlings suggested that we all take a chill pill. I said that I did not want any kind of pills without checking to see if they are on the Banned Substances List. Prince Charles asked if it was homoeopathic. Tomas said he had a packet of mints that were his favourite, he held out his hand offering us one each and as we each took turns in taking one he asked us all what our favourite Queen song was.

Mr Bradlings said his was 'Bo Rap' to which I corrected him advising that Queen did not sing Rap songs and he must be thinking about M and Ms.

"What have you been drinking GOAT? You been on the cider tonight?" he said.

The evening was getting tiresome, "No Mr. Bradlings, I do not drink anything other than Champagne and Lemonade Shandy."

Andrew of the Murrays said, "Thirty Nine."

"I am not thirty nine! I was born in 1981," I really felt like going homes at this point.

Tom said that it actually was the name of a Queen song and that it was very good. I do like Tomas, but could not help thinking that he and Andrew were trying to pull the wool over My eyes.

I gestured to everyone to shut up. That noise up ahead was there again and now I thought I saw a shadow moving in the same direction as where the noise was.

Mr. Bradlings whispered that Queen's Greatest Hits album was recognised in 2012 as the best selling UK album of all time. He also mentioned that one of his favourite bands was Metallica and that he is friends with their drummer, Lars Ulrich. His Royal Highness Prince Charles said Metallica was a little too loud for One and that he much preferred the melodic tones of The Carpenters, to which he then started singing, Top of The World. I must admit that it was a little difficult not to join in so I started doing the hummings and the wiggling of the feet.

Andrew asked if he could go home as this was getting a bit silly.

Then suddenly everybody stopped and froze as they all saw the shadow too, there it was clearly visible just ahead of us. Could it be Mr. Wimbledon playing the tricks on us? For that matter, could it be Hawkeye? Tom looked through the lens of the thermal imaging camera and said that there was certainly something moving there. Andrew flicked the switch on the EMF meter and said the readings were definitely higher than they should have been. I took My temperature and it was normal.

We edged closer to the strange phenomenon, holding our breath in the anticipations. Could it really be a ghost? The hairs were standing up on the back of My neck, legs, back, chest, arms and toes. I was really feeling very anxious. I called out, "Hello? Are you a ghost?"

Andrew burst out laughing, "Did you really just say that to a ghost? Ghosts don't know that they are ghosts."

I snapped at him, "How would you know what ghosts feel?" I could not take it any longer and lunged at the Wimbledon trophy grabbing it trying to pull it away, "It is Mine, give it back to Me." I wanted it, how dare he claim ownership of what was rightfully Mine.

After a short grapple Tom pulled Me away saying, "Let it be, let it be, there will be an answer, let it be." I thanked him for his words of wisdom and told him that he is still a light that shines on Me when I find Myself in times of trouble.

We all looked ahead as the shadow quickly moved from the corridor and through a gangway into Centre Court. Prince Charles yelled authoritatively, "Halt, who goes there? Friend or Foe?"

Andrew politely reminded the Prince that nobody actually speaks like that any more.

We ventured into gangway G where we saw the apparition disappear into just a moment ago. After climbing the steps an army officer asked Me for My ticket, I showed him My pass and said I usually like to sit in row B, seat 15. He politely directed Me to My seat which really was very nice of him. I turned around to tell him that I had always thought that the Service Personnel always do a wonderful job but he had disappeared. I fell silent. Where had he gone? For that matter, where were the team? I could not even hear Mr. Bradlings any more so I knew they were not nearby. But where were they? They were behind Me just a moment ago. I was not sure what to do. If I left My seat somebody else may take it. I looked around and recognised the famous court's characteristics. Even though it was the middle of the night it was almost a full moon which allowed you to see the brilliance of Centre Court. I felt nostalgic and a little tear began to swell up from one of My eyes.

Suddenly I heard scuffling sounds from across the court. I could see something moving in the Royal Box but it was too dark to recognise anything. Was it Sir Cliff Richard or another member of the Royal family? I called out, "Hello?" The court lights came on and I saw the rest of the gang pointing and laughing at Me. I shouted to them, "You are not allowed in the Royal box, get out before I call Mr. Wimbledon!"

Tomas Berdych yelled back, "Frankie said relax, don't do it."

I checked through the contacts on My portable telephone and did not have anybody named Frankie listed. I do know a Frank but it is My second cousin and I did not think Tomas knew him. Andrew and Tomas were behaving like children hitting each other with the rather comfortable complimentary cushions supplied as standard in the Royal box. Mr. Bradlings appeared to be enjoying a glass of champagne whilst Mr. Charles was cupping a steaming hot cup of cocoa which apparently he enjoys every evening before bed, at around half past eight. Looks like we had something in common.

I made My way weaving through the seats to where they were and asked them what happened to the gentleman that asked for My ticket and whether they saw him. Andrew scoffed that there was nobody there and it was all part of My imagination.

Tomas said, "They seek him here, they seek him there. His clothes are loud but never square."

I was a little confused, there *was* somebody there, I spoke to him, saw him with My own eyes and he certainly did not have any Kinks in his suit.

I felt like I was the only one taking this seriously and I certainly did not appreciate the lack of respect being shown in the Royal box. I called to the others to make their way out and to meet Me at the front of the building. Mr. Bradlings said he had to go to the hotel and check in with the ESPN team on the West Coast. I asked him if he wanted us to walk him there but he slapped Me on the back, a little harder than I expected, said he would be fine and exclaimed, "Goodnight GOAT." Prince Charles said it was way past his bed time and that he should go too. Andrew and Tomas said they also wanted to get back as they wanted to play video games.

Suddenly I was alone at 3:30am. Would it have hurt them to have stayed a little longer? I thought we were having the fun times. Even My staff had abandoned Me. I felt lost and vulnerable. I decided to go for a walk around the outside courts to see if I could see that shadow or ghost again, unless it was never a ghost and one of them playing the tricks on Me, I was determined to find out. I turned left out of Centre Court, past gate five and stood by the champagne bar. Everything was neat and tidy. If you have been to Wimbledon you will know that the little food area opposite the outside bars has the floor painted like a tennis court. It is quite exciting really but sadly cannot be used for tournaments. Still, I am grateful that it is not clay. The silence was broken with what sounded like musicians tuning their instruments. I know that there is a live band usually playing further up from where I was standing but what were they doing here in the middle of the night?

PSEUDOFED

Perhaps somebody told them I would be there, that would explain it.

I continued walking towards where the band sit when the music stopped suddenly. I climbed the steps up to the next level to get a better view and saw that the band area was empty, so where did the music come from? Just ahead of Me was the famous statue of top fashion designer Fred Perry. It was lit up as usual. It is a nice statue but I really do not think it belongs there, it is not like he played tennis or anything. I saw the Wimbledon shop ahead of Me and to My right the doors were open. As I walked in someone kindly offered Me a basket and wished Me a lovely day which was nice. The store itself was rather pleasant with different clothes, sports equipment (mainly tennis) and some little souvenirs. A lovely rose coloured sweater caught My eye. I checked to see if they had My size and they did but it was the last one so I hurriedly put it in My basket. Wandering around I remembered the Wimbledon jam, or as My American fans call it, jelly. It is so delicious but they always seem to run out after the first week which makes Me do the irritated faces. I was hoping to find some but was unsuccessful, the shelves were empty. I went to the counter and a nice lady took My new sweater, folded it neatly and asked Me if I was having a lovely day to which I replied that I was. She asked if I was interested in a pair of Wimbledon sunglasses which apparently were the

'Umpires' Choice'. Well, judging by some of the calls made against Me they were the last thing I needed, so politely declined.

I left the shop making the chuffed faces pleased with the sweater I had just bought. I turned right and decided to head towards Number One Court. There is a big scoreboard on the way there to the left but I decided to ignore it, 2013 was not a vintage year. Up ahead and to the right I thought I saw something move. I called out but there was no reply. If this was Andrew of the Murrays again making fun of Me I swear I will get staff to swing for him. The dark shadow was near the other food court almost under Number One court. I quickened My pace and directed My feet to where I thought I saw the figure. When I arrived there was nobody there, it was empty, just tables and chairs where normal people sit outside and eat the snacks they had just purchased or the little sandwiches that they bought themselves from home. Maybe it was My eyes and I had been seeing things all along and there were no shadows? No, I dismissed this as impossible. I have twenty twenty vision and My eyes are regularly tested by My Orthodontist.

There was a sound in the food area itself so I ventured over, almost jogging. I looked at the menu at Hot Wok and suddenly felt an appetite growing inside the tummy.

A voice said, "Can I help?"

I looked around but could not see anybody, I leaned over the counter to see if somebody was crouching but there was nobody.

"Hello, what can I get you today?" the voice said again.

Feeling the hunger games I asked for vegetable noodles. I looked down and there it was, a cardboard take-out style box. Delicious! I walked back to the cutlery and sauces counter and took a fork. It was made of plastic. Was this somebody's idea of the joke? I certainly was not laughing. Who eats using this? I prized open the container and was hit by the fragrant aroma of the noodles. I gave the box a second look as it seemed to be half the size of the previous years. I think Mr. Wimbledon was doing the sneaky faces with the profits. As I tucked into the noodles My eyes looked up to the flat screen televisions that usually show live scores. They were switched on displaying the score of the final between Novak and Andrew, I tried to look away but the picture became distorted as though the television was losing its connection. I looked around and the other televisions located nearby were behaving the same way. Suddenly they went black and a message started scrolling across the screen in red text, it read, 'Hello GOAT'.

I stopped chewing, noodles halfway out of My mouth and a piece of broccoli fell onto My shirt on its way down and then rolled onto the ground. It was quite upsetting as you are lucky if you get one piece of broccoli to begin with. The stain of soy sauce on My shirt was even more annoying. I felt anxious in case I would run into Anna Winterbottom. What would she say?

The message on the screen scrolled from right to left and as I watched the nice salutation disappear, a new message appeared, 'Run'. I quickly looked in both directions expecting to see another ball whizzing past Me just out of reach but Rafaello was nowhere to be seen. I think this was just GTSD, GOAT Traumatic Stress Disorder. The screen above flickered, a new message scrolled across, 'I said RUN!'. I put down the box of noodles, quickly unzipped My bag and looked for My running shoes. I slipped into them and changed from My sweatpants into a crisp pair of white shorts. I tied My laces and grabbed a drink from the bag, it was lemon flavoured water with a twist of mint that I always carry around with Me in case I have to play more than three sets. I was ready, My heart was beating quickly and so was My brain. Which was the quickest way out, left or right? I saw what appeared to be a crowd of shadow people from the right moving towards Me, almost gliding slightly above the ground. Had they just come from the shop nearby?

I smiled at them, "Hi guys, do you know if there is any strawberries and cream left?" No answer, they kept moving in My direction, "Looking for an autograph or some selfie photos with Me?" I shouted in a friendly voice.

There was something distinctly odd looking about them, I felt a little scared, why were they all moving as one and where were their feet? I calculated that there was not enough room to run past them to the right. Anyhow, this would take Me into the middle of the grounds again and towards the BBC Studios increasing the chances of running into the presenter, Sue Barker. A voice inside My left ear told Me to run to the left and not to stop, the voice inside My right ear was not sure which direction to go. I grabbed My things, including the bag containing the stylish garment I had just bought, and ran. These legs have got a few years left in them. I was too scared to look back. The gate was just ahead, hopefully I would find one of those lovely Honorary Stewards who would help Me out.

I felt dizzy, My head was spinning around and around like a record baby. My knees stopped working, the mind started to fear, was I playing Rafaello again? I felt Myself falling…

I woke up the next morning in a lovely warm bed, the memories of the night before started rushing through the brain. Someone was licking My face repeatedly. Had

Sue Barker caught up with Me after all? I sat up quickly and saw two doggy fans looking at Me. There was a knock on the bedroom door, I thought it was a little too early for the postman although I was waiting for a delivery of scented candles from the Shopping Channel. They had a special offer the previous week where if you buy two sets, you get free delivery. I pulled the sheet up over My chest and said, "Come in."

"You all right, Man?" It was Andrew of the Murrays, still with that grin, but somehow I was relieved to see him as he sat on the side of the bed.

"What happened?" I asked.

"We got a call from the local Police saying that you had collapsed outside the grounds during the night so we came to pick you up and brought you over to the house."

"Did they mention the ghosts?" I asked.

He smirked, "There were no ghosts, GOAT, there is no such thing."

"Did I have a shopping bag with Me?"

"What? Of course you didn't. Why would you have a shopping bag with you in the middle of the night in the Wimbledon grounds?"

PSEUDOFED

He stood up and said he was going to take the dogs for a walk and that I could get up in My own time, he mentioned that there were fresh towels in the guest bathroom and some food downstairs. Kim called to Andrew from downstairs to hurry the $%&! up or she was going to leave without him so he went. I waited until I heard them shut the front door before getting up. I peered out of the window and saw the British countryside, pleasant as always. I wanted to shower before Andrew and Kim returned and I was not sure what time room service ended so thought I had better hurry. Walking out of the bedroom carrying some essentials in a bag I began to hope Andrew's house was not as large as My homes. For the convenience of guests I have maps located at various points with those, 'You are here' signs so they can find their way around. I doubt Andrew had thought of this. I mean, where are the fire exits in this place? This is a homes isn't it? Where are the restaurants and gift shops? I tried the door across the small hallway and it was a bathroom. It had most things I needed: basin, bidet, bath with separate jacuzzi and walk-in shower. I noticed a beautiful picture he had on the wall then realised it was a mirror. I smiled. As I looked around I froze, Andrew had Wimbledon towels! I quickly retrieved My portable telephone and took pictures as evidence, wait until I tell Mr. Wimbledon.

The walk-in shower was adequate though I noticed you had to walk out of the same area that you use to walk in which seemed odd. There was only one type of shampoo and conditioner available which was disconcerting and I remember hoping that My scalp would not flare up and itch for the rest of the day. I looked around for a clay face mask but there was not any available. I made a mental note so I could leave an appropriate review on Trips Advisor when getting back homes.

Going downstairs and into the kitchen there was a selection of cakes on the table with an envelope propped up against the teapot. It had 'GOAT' written across it. I looked around for a letter opener but could not see one, nor could I see any staff, how was I supposed to open it? Feeling a little irritated I sat down and chose a slice of the Victoria Sponge cake. It was very tasty and I am sure it had a hint of liqueur. I remembered the events of the previous night, I *had* seen ghosts, I know I had.

As I wiped the mouth with a napkin My portable telephone vibrated once, text message. I flipped it open to see Sue Barker inviting Me to her house for dinner. I turned the phone off quickly and removed the battery.

By the time I got to the end of the cake I heard the key in the door, it was Andrew, Kim and the doggy fans. They all came into the kitchen and both wished Me a good morning.

Kim noticed that I had already had some cake and said, "Did you enjoy it? They are just &%$£ing delicious aren't they?"

I was not sure how to reply so just said, "Yes, thank you".

Andrew looked at the envelope, "Aren't You going to open it?"

"I couldn't find your letter opener," I said, obviously.

Kim laughed and said, "What the %&$£? That's hilarious GOAT, tell me you are $%&£ing joking."

Andrew looked at Me puzzled and declared, "Just open it with your hands," as he picked it up using his fingers to tear down the seam.

As he did this I looked at him curiously with My head slightly tilted to one side. I noticed the doggies looking at Me in the same way. He handed Me the note contained in the envelope and I opened it. It was from

Judy of the Murrays and read, 'Hope you enjoy the cakes Pseudolicious. I have seen the ghosts too.'

I felt a huge sense of relief and did not feel alone any more. Judy made the confirmations that she had seen them as well. We were now bonded for life, BFFFs. As I sat quietly pondering this thought, a song entered into the head, "If there's something strange, in your neighbourhood. Who ya gonna call?..."

Andrew, Kim and the doggies were all staring at Me, "What the %&*$ PF? Are you OK?" Kim asked.

I raised My head, looked at her, smiled and said, "The GOAT ain't afraid of no ghosts."

8

THE POWER OF NOT NOW

Spiritual GOAT Quote:
"Two wrongs sometimes make a right."

— PF xx

If you have ever looked into the spirituality you probably have come across the importance of staying in the present moment, sometimes this is also referred to as mindfulness. Sometimes we hear other players talk about this too. They refer to the importance of trying to remain 'present', especially during an important point or during rest breaks when you are a set down. How do they know such things? Well, either somebody told them or it looks as though they read books in between matches, unlike Me, I do not read them, I write them. You're welcome.

Let us examine it more closely, what is this being mindful all about and why is it apparently important? The theory is that most of us live day by day on memories or thinking about the future and in doing so you are missing the present moment. For the examples, I am sure we have all thought about and had the excitement of when we just cannot wait for the next dwelling to be built after having had the final meeting with the architect. It is an exciting time as we look forward to another place we can call homes. When I say I am sure that we have all thought about it, you and I both know that I am not referring to you. The theory of mindfulness tells us that thinking in this way is incorrect. It suggests that we can certainly be happy with looking forward but the focus should be on the *now* most of the time because after all, it is all you have, apparently.

Another example of this is when we look at one area in the sports psychologies. This tells us staying in the present moment can be the difference between winning and choosing to lose. I am certain we have all seen those matches when a little guy is receiving on match point or even serving for the match. It is potentially the big win for them. Then suddenly their mind does the rememberings and they realise what they could achieve if they win the next point. This will be a momentous time and could well be the turning point that they have been waiting their whole life for this. All those endless hours in the gym, all those flights taken around the world, those moments daydreaming of being a champion. Going through a phase of growing their hair a little longer so they can look like Me, or in Andre Agassi's case, just attaching the hair extensions. All these thoughts and images flashing through the mind as they are standing on the baseline bouncing the ball, the crowd falls silent. They think, what do I do now? Do I serve a little different than I have been throughout the whole match? Who is watching? Everybody! Then as they look across the net preparing to toss the ball in the air they see Me, the GOAT. Sure I did a few shankings, generously peppered with some unforced errors to be on the wrong side of match point, however, I still show the serious faces, especially to the little guys. In this moment the little guy is thinking about every movement during the serve motion, something that should be just automatic and that he has done thousands of times before. His muscles get a little tighter due to being nervous, he strikes the ball and it lands in the net while I do the smiling faces. Some people refer to this as the chokings. The job of the sports psychologist will be to help the little guy not think about these things and to stay in the moment and look at the next serve in terms of it being just another point.

My take on focusing on the now? False. There is nothing in the present moment and I will prove it to you. Now. What just happened? Nothing. Shall we try again? Now. Still nothing. You see, nothing actually happens in the now other than you interrupting something that can be quite pleasant. I could be enjoying a scrumptious bruncheon that Chef kindly prepared and the last thing I want to do is stop eating it just to think about what? Eating it? I was doing that already.

You have to agree, this makes no sense. Let us say you are about to serve for your seventeenth Grand Slam, would you really stop thinking about it and pretend you are just serving for the first round match against a little guy, a mere mortal who is much lesser than you? Well, we both know I mean Me. No, the mere idea of this would be incorrect and a lie and it is bad to tell the lies, look at what happened to Mr. Pinocchio's nose when he did not say the truthfulness. If you tried to pretend that match point was a serve in the first set of a less important match you would be very shocked as the ace ball swept passed your opponent and everybody would be doing the cheerings. Why are they cheering so loudly you would ask yourself? And in *this* moment you would not do the obligatory celebrations that you *should* be doing. Imagine the photographs in the newspapers the following day, rather than looking victorious, the headlines would ask why you look so confused. Not only that, if you pretended that it was the beginning of a less important match as you are about to serve for the championship you would probably also start to be very worried and would ask yourself why you feel so tired. Think about it, you have only just started this match, in your head, yet it feels like you have been playing three hours! Well silly, that is because you have been playing for three hours. You see, do not lie to yourself, let alone anybody else. You are about to serve probably the biggest point of your career and yes, it could very well change your life forever. If you are unable to serve it out it simply means you are not good enough.

Now… Still nothing.

The other big part of spirituality talks about being happy and content with what you have. The idea is that while you are constantly searching for something you forget to appreciate what you already have. In addition, when you finally get that something, perhaps a new yacht or another homes, you are still not happy because you then move on and want something else, like perhaps a private jet or a bigger garage for your cars. So the whole time what you are actually doing is chasing and wanting something that, when you get it, does not make you happy after all. Again, they also say that by doing this you miss being in the *now* but we already know how that one goes.

Now… Still nothing.

Does any of this make sense to Me? No, not at all. I already appreciate what I have, thank you for asking and yes, I am hungry for more. If you did not wish for things like the latest portable telephone or perhaps an expensive timepiece, how could you possibly be happy? If you went to the supermarket how would you know to buy champagne if you had not wished for it? The champagne does not come to you, well, unless you ordered it using homes delivery but you still had to have wanted it to begin with otherwise you would not have known what to order. Well, actually, staff would have ordered it but you would have needed to tell them that you wanted it, so you follow My way of thinking on this. Let us toss this theory aside too. To make the summaries, do not stay in the present moment and yes, always wish for things.

I remember in 2008 at Roland Garros where I had big plans to win that year. Paris is always a lovely place for Me and staff. You get up nice and early in the hotel, put on something casual like a nice pair of freshly pressed trousers, perhaps a matching shirt, everyday cuff links and then decide how you are going to wear one of your fine silk scarfs. Sometimes I just hang it around the neck and throw one end over one of My shoulders, other times I tie opposite corners and wear it more like a shawl, it really depends on the mood I am in. Of course, no stay in the French capital is complete without the obligatory beret. My choice is the Blancq-Olibet beret as it is a lot like Me, timeless and classic.

On the day of the final I ventured out very early and went to My favourite boulangerie to pick up a little something for breakfast. Yes, of course, usually this activity is either carried out by staff or the owner of the boulangerie, a pleasant little French man, who delivers it to the hotel and leaves it outside the door of My suite first thing in the morning. However, I encourage you to do as I do and sometimes do things for yourself. Not too often but occasionally. It really keeps your feet on the ground, although I suspect this is more due to gravity than humility.

I was the first customer in the shop that day and the smell of freshly baked bread and pastries consumed the senses in My head. My mouth was starting to make the salivations and I realised what it felt like to be a doggy. I quickly ran in and put My front paws on the counter, barking in excitement and no matter how hard the owner, Guillaume, tried to calm Me, I would not sit. As I had been residing here for over two weeks that year, he already had My package ready, two pain au chocolat. I asked him to throw in some chocolate pastries too as it was finals day. I wished him a bonjour and left eagerly heading back to the hotel. Coming here year after year, the same hotel and always frequenting the same baker, I was able to find My way back on My own.

It is quite nice dressing like a local and being able to speak the regional accent as not many people bother you for autographs and those selfie photos. Goodness knows how many fans have taken pictures with Me and with today's technologies and the wireless gadgets, they can post a picture of Me on the social media sites within that very same week! Extraordinary, what will they think of next?

After staff watched Me eat breakfast, we had the transport organised to take us to the venue and practice courts so I could hit My balls in preparations for the final. Here lies the real world example of everything I have spoken about so far. Was I in the present moment? No, in My mind I was actually already having the victory dinner. The correct side of sports psychology tells you to do the visualisations, to picture in your mind what you already want and to think it through as though you have achieved it. This is where I was that morning, there was nothing in the present moment. I was hungry for it, even so soon after breakfast. I was not focusing on the now nor was I content with what I already had achieved which was merely just a place in the final. Anybody can get one of those. Because I felt that I had already won, I did not want a strenuous training session, what was the point? As soon as I felt the stinging in the eyes from the first bead of sweat I signalled to staff that training was over. They looked a little surprised but they know better than to question.

Venturing into the locker rooms I took a quick shower just to freshen up before the pre-match media obligations. The first was with Mats Winglander and I can assure you that I am never mindful in his interviews. I am far from content with what I have in that moment, all I want is for it to finish. I know that there are very keen fans that go to incredible lengths to see Me, but Mats takes it to the next level of fan dedication. He has sent Me his résumé countless times and always seems to be in the most unexpected places. I remember once sitting at homes during the off-season (one day in December) when I felt as though I needed to quench My thirst. I sauntered over to the refrigerator, activated the iris security feature to unlock and opened it and Mats was inside and handed Me the lemonade. I thanked him and closed the door but it took some moments to elapse to realise what just happened. Despite this, in Paris during the interview I was professional and polite as always. The same went for all the press conferences that day, in eighteen languages, excluding Spanish. I assertively stated that I was going to win and I had every reason to think it. In My mind of course, I had already won.

As the time got nearer I saw people around Me getting both excited and nervous. *They* were in the present moment! Moi? I was cool, calm and relaxed, after all, I was already the champion and was more worried about what to have for dessert in the celebratory evening meal. I dare say that if I was mindful, about to play Rafaello, the long-haired boy who beat Me the very first time we played in Miami in 2004, I may have been concerned too, but not this time. As the great philosopher, Chesney Hawkes, once said:

> "I am the one and only
> Nobody I'd rather be
> I am the one and only
> You can't take that away from Me."

Incidentally, I can make the confirmations that Mr. C. Hawkes is by no means related to Hawkeye. I did the research and double checked on Ancestry.com, though I must say that this was a little bit annoying as I had to pay for a subscription to get all the information and now I have access for a year. I am not even sure if it renews automatically.

The moment had arrived, the final. As we walked out onto the court I acknowledged the crowd briefly. No matter what, the Parisians love Me, as well they should. As I was playing Rafaello, I knew we had about forty five minutes before the warm up so I sat down on one of the chairs and made Myself comfortable placing a small cushion, that I had in My bag, behind Me on the backrest. I gestured a ball servant to throw Me a banana. I began to eat it making sure not to make eye contact with anyone and was careful to chew it well to aid digestion. Also in My bag I had some chilled alcohol-free Baby Cham, why not start the celebrations early, n'est-ce pas?

PSEUDOFED

After enjoying the snacks I decided to walk up to the net and wait for Rafaello after all. I looked over to where he was sitting and saw him trying furiously to squeeze the contents of a small sachet straight into his mouth. He does that before every match and I still do not understand why he finds it so difficult. His knees were jumping up and down quickly as though they were attached to the electricity cables. Just for a second I was brought back into the now, the present moment and I felt the nervousness in My tummies. I shook My head and snapped Myself out of it. I remembered I had already won this match. Eventually he got up and seemed to leap to where I was waiting with Mr. Umpire. I could already hear the television commentators talking about how he lines up the water bottles, again. He seemed taller than I remember, I try to avoid him whenever possible, especially nowadays. Why could he not stand still while Mr. Umpire was reading the rules and talking about tossing the coin? He is always fidgeting. I had to remind Myself that it did not matter, in the large scheme of things I was the French Open champion of 2008 and it felt good. Just before we went to the baseline to start the warm up, Nadal asked to have a couple of photographs taken with Me over the net which was quite nice.

The first set began and My mind was on whether I had put the towels on the bathroom floor in the hotel in order to get a fresh set. Sometimes I forget and it is so annoying. Again, should I be content to even have towels in the first place? No, everybody needs towels otherwise we would never be dry. Come to think of it, did I set the code to the in-room safe? Was it 1981 or 2008? After about half an hour the Umpire said I had lost the first set 6-1. A little rude given that we need to define what losing actually means and we had not yet discussed this. What is so wrong with 6-1? In many cultures the number one actually means best. After all, is it better to be the number one seedling or number six? I rest My case.

I felt relaxed during the set break and tried to keep an expressionless face. I was squinting a little, though My mind was well and truly dialled into the future. The next slam would be at Mr. Wimbledon's house in just a few short weeks and I was certainly looking forward to that. I had not yet announced that I would be wearing an absolutely gorgeous off-white cardigan as part of My official outfit with a matching pair of flappy long shorts. Who needs the *now* when you have all this? I looked over to My team to send them a little wave and the smiling faces in case any of them were taking photos. One or two of them were gesturing that I should stay focused by pointing at their eyes. There is nothing wrong with My eyes thank you very much, I thought. In addition, should I require spectacles in the future, I have already decided that I will probably purchase a monocle. I rummaged through My bag for

PSEUDOFED

My portable telephone to check Twitter. I wanted to check if the person who does My parody account had done any courtside tweetings during the match but I could not find the phone, perhaps I left it at the hotel. I was starting to get a little headache and reached for some PseudoFed.

I strutted over to the baseline and nodded that I was ready to receive the serve. I felt good. History had already been written long before this match had started and I was recognised as the Greatest Player Of All Time, also known as the GOAT. The end result was, therefore, quite meaningless. What would I do with the prize money? I checked scores and it suggested it was Me to serve. Odd, I thought Rafaello served first in this set? Oh he had, the game was already over. At this point in the match I had not won a single point on the second serve so thought I had better just stick to the first serve. I bounced the ball a few times, looking down I noticed My socks were dirty from this horrid clay, it really is so uncivilised and pre-historic to play on. Is this how Frederick Flintstone started out his tennis career? Time has moved on and so should we. I know players often change shirts during the break but I was even wondering if I could change socks. I decided against it as I did not want anybody looking at My ankles. By the end of the set I felt I did OK, 6-3 down which was a three hundred percent improvement on the first set. Statistics anyone should be proud of.

Sitting down I was not sure what to do during this break. The crowd were very quiet, more than usual. I remembered that I was thinking about the present moment so I snapped out of it slapping Myself around the face with a swift forehand. Wow, something else I was good at! Lucky it was not My backhand, I might have missed. I thought ahead to the next tournament, the Jerry Springer Open. The stadium is a bit boxy but Jerry always welcomes Me with flowers and chocolates. I had a good feeling about that tournament too and at least it is on grass. The only thing I am not too sure about going there each year is that I have a lifetime contraction to play. I signed it but nobody had made the clarifications as to what this exactly meant. Do I have to play there for the rest of My life? This answers the question people ask about why I have not retired yet, I am literally unable to as I am under contract with Jerry.

I changed My shirt and considered unwrapping a croissant that I had in My bag. I found the chic espresso sized flask too and the miniature cup, however, the matching saucer was nowhere to be found. I looked across to the team looking very agitated, someone should have packed it. One of them looked back mouthing something that looked like, 'What are you doing?'. What did they think I was doing? Sometimes staff need reminding their place in the order of the pecking and this was one of those times. Accept and be happy that I have staff to begin with? No, never appreciate a necessity in life. Expect more. How was I supposed to drink without the saucer? Where would I place the little cup?

I looked up and realised that the third set had started without Me. This was a little surprising but on reflection allowed the conservation of energy, we must all do what we can to help save the planet. I got up and thought I had better join in, the fans had paid with their little wallets after all. I nodded to the ball servants for three balls which I balanced on the racquet. I am never quite sure which one to give back. I see other players always asking for three, looking at them and then tossing one away but how do they know which one? I looked carefully, determined to find something but they all looked the same. I tried using the mathematical formula called eenie meenie miney moe and found that this did not help at all as I kept forgetting which one I started with. I opted for the other method, O-U-T spells out and this quickly helped choose the ball to give back. Maybe this is what the other players do? Having two left I put one in My pocket and walked carefully to the baseline. Lifting one foot I struck the sole of the shoe with the racquet and a cloud of that disgusting filthy clay released itself from in between the tread on My tennis shoes. I could not wait for the match to be over and *was* looking forward to the end. I bounced the ball a couple of times looking up to see where the Spanish one was standing and hesitated, where was he? I looked over to the chairs and saw he was sitting down as three games had already passed. Great! The sooner we get this match over with the sooner I get on Fed Force One and fly back homes.

After the match everybody seemed so down and solemn. I asked a couple of journalists what had happened but they did not really reply, one put his hand on My shoulder and gave a smile that was sincere yet felt sad. I smiled back. It was one of the most surreal moments of My career and to this day I still do not know why everybody was so upset. *This* is the price they paid for being in the present moment. Me? I had completely managed the match and got off that horrible antiquated surface in less than two hours! Who was the real Victor… Hanescu?

This is a fine example of learning to think for yourself. Be your own guru, there is no need to learn from anybody else. If you had followed other people's teachings and you were Me, and I can confirm that you certainly are not, you would have tried hard to focus on every moment during the match which would have made it seem twice as long. You also would have been distraught upon having lost. But what is losing? This brings us to the next important subject of the perceptions.

9

THE PSYCHOLOGY OF THE PERCEPTIONS

Spiritual GOAT Quote:
"Always hold onto your dignity, better still, ask staff to do it for you."

— PF xx

Now you must sit comfortably, ask staff to remove any chewing gum from your mouth and no talking please. It is like the school times except what I am about to teach you is far more important. We will talk and make the discussions about the subject of psychology. What is this? It is the study of the mind, brain and head. One aspect of psychology is that of perception. A little known fact is that it actually used to be called deception. You may think you already know what the perception is and so you believe that there is nothing more to say about this subject but you do not and there is.

If I show you a picture of a tree, what will you see? Let us put aside the different types of trees that exist in the nature, just think of a tree. What do you think about it? You probably think that it is just a tree and it is boring. Where does your opinion come from? It comes from your head. It may shock you to know that everybody has a different head and no matter what the experience the head has had or indeed the type of picture the eyes are looking at, everybody perceives something different and personal each and every time we see something. I shall make the elaborations as you probably have little idea what I am saying. If you were a lumberjack person you may wonder how much money this tree can make you after you chop it down with your rather large axe. If you were a furniture maker you may think of the lumberjack person because you would be thinking of the wonderful tables and chairs you can make from this tree and you need the lumberjack to do the choppings for you. If you were a little squirrel fan you may look at the tree as a nice homes for the family or perhaps a vacation villa. If you were a doggy fan you may look at the tree and see it as a toilet. You see the points I am making for you? What you should have noticed is that even though you all see a tree, you all perceive something different when you do the seeings. Actually if we want to take this one set further, a tree is a name that we have chosen to give this object in this particular type of language we are using to make the communications. If the person that first thought of the word 'tree' had called this very big plant a GOAT, then it would still smell and feel the same and a doggy fan would still have the urge to raise its leg when it saw the GOAT. Equally, when you see Me walk on court, you would all be thinking, look at that lovely tree about to play tennis, what beautiful branches he has.

What we learn from this psychological subject of the fascinations is that there are two things happening. The first is what your senses pick up. Our senses are sight, taste, touch, smell, hearing and hair. When there is a noise, like the whisper of My feet as I barely touch the court efficiently gliding from one side to the other, the sound that I make is real, there is only one sound as it travels through the air causing the good vibrations. Your ears are alerted to this and they eat the sound using the ear drum closely followed by the tiny bones in your ear; the hammer, anvil and the stirrups. The second thing that happens next is that once inside the head your brain acknowledges the sound, says thank you, and decides what the sound is. How does it do this? By using a special filing system, a little like a library, it checks along all the shelves of stored knowledge you already have, pacing up and down, until it finds a match. It then takes this book to the counter and asks the librarian how long it can be borrowed for. You must appreciate these two stages, the first is the action itself which is constant and has nothing to do with perception. The second is the library stage, let us refer to this as the head library from now on. The point being is not that we each have a library in the head, it is that the library is different for each and every one of us. No two head libraries are the same; your head library is probably quite small and has a few shelves of dusty books and video cassettes to choose from. My head library is grand, has plush carpets and an elevator to each floor packed with endless shelves of informations and dozens of staff members that know where everything is. In addition, if there is a book I need the staff members can download it at a moment's notice.

From this we begin to understand something else. This is that the head library is used whether you like it or not. You have no choice whatsoever. You cannot, for example, see Me on the television set and not have a reaction. Your head library will tell you it is Me and there is nothing you can do about it. Should you have a head library malfunction, ensure you have the volume up as the wonderful commentators will certainly remind you of how great I am every few minutes. The fact that you have no choice in this is rather clever, it means your head is always trying to finish a sentence, trying to use the little knowledge you have to predict the outcome of a situation or complete a story that you have only been told part of. Imagine if I begin to draw a picture of a tennis racquet with a pencil but I do not quite finish. I have drawn the handle, the frame and begin to sketch the net but stop half way through leaving a hole. You will not scratch your head wondering what it is, you will already know that it is a tennis racquet. It will be the same if I draw a hexagon and only draw five lines instead of six leaving a gap, you will make the assumption faces thinking it is an unfinished hexagonal shape. Of course, for both of these examples you must have already known what a tennis racquet and hexagon is to begin with and this is an important aspect. Remember that everything is stored in your head library.

For Me, the most important thing this helps us understand is that when you talk, the words that come out of your mouth originate from your head library. Given this is uniquely yours as we have discussed, as the person you are talking to hears the words you speak, their own head library is used to understand what you say. So it is very likely that even though you and your friend believe you agree on something, you are both thinking something completely different using the same set of words.

Here is a transcript of an interview I gave that illustrates My point. It took place a couple of days after one of My many Grand Slam Wimbledon victories in 2012.

The exclusive interview was recorded for a large television network and the appointment was in central London at one of the big hotels you have probably never been in, let alone stayed at. My car arrived in good time and the little man waiting outside the main door approached the car and opened the door to let Me out. He had a very tall immaculate top hat and looked like he had just walked off a 1930s movie set. I remember admiring the hat wondering if I could obtain a white one for My next Wimbledon tournament. He opened the door and greeted Me to which I acknowledged his formality. From the car, I skipped over to the hotel door that was already being held open by somebody or other, that was their job. Can you imagine? I can't. Once inside a nice lady approached and shook My hand. She led us over through the foyer to a hallway and into a room that had already been prepared for the interview. I had to go through make-up although before anybody makes the laughing faces at Me for this, it is quite normal to have staff type people put powder on the face before going on camera. It reduces the shiny look and gives a lovely matte finish that is appealing to the eye as well as working well on camera.

I was led to a chair that I am sure had been sat in before which made me do the hesitation faces. I placed My bottoms down in the seat and made Myself comfortable crossing one leg over the other, and then again over the other. The trouser-leg bottom came up somewhat high and some skin was showing above the sock, I hurriedly pulled it down before the interviewer came over.

What I am going to illustrate here is how two people can have a very pleasant conversation yet they are in totally different sections of their individual head libraries. I was thinking about the night before when I went to the theatre in London to see the top hit musical, Mamma Mia. I was making the assumptions that this is what the questions were about and yet the interviewer was referring to two days before when I won My seventeenth Grand Slam title.

The interview started as they usually do, making the introduction highlighting the accolades, achievements and staff, "Welcome PseudoFed and thank you so much for taking the time to come and talk to us, Wimbledon Champion!"

"Yes," I acknowledged with the big Swiss-cheesy grin and looking rather pleased with Myself.

"Wow that was quite a show," she said excitedly.

"Thank you, yes, it really was. All the fans there, it was such a wonderful atmosphere, I really enjoyed it."

I think she was a little nervous, "Erm, did you ever feel the outcome was in doubt?"

I paused a moment before replying, an old trick I had learned that creates tension and excitement during interviews, "Well, I was not quite sure of the outcome to be honest with you but it really was thrilling from start to finish."

She referred to her notes, "What was your favourite part?"

"I think the moves were so amazing and it was obvious everybody involved had trained and practised really hard, it was quite a performance and I will not forget it any time soon."

"Wow really?" she asked, "Why did this one feel so special?"

I knew the answer, "The main difference between this one and the others was that all the way through I just felt like I wanted to burst out singing!"

She looked puzzled although I was not sure why, "Singing? I certainly did not expect you to say that. You really must have been enjoying yourself."

"Yes I was, I nearly started dancing at one stage."

"Oh goodness, right there shows the level of confidence you had," she said.

"Well, it was not so much about confidence but more about the rhythm," I explained.

Her face went a little more serious, "Yes finding the rhythm is really important isn't it. Is this what you guys refer to as being in the zone?"

"I don't know, I really was just having fun." I said.

"Well, it was certainly exciting to watch to be honest with you."

"You were there too? I didn't see you. What time did you arrive?" It was not the first time she had interviewed Me so I think I would have recognised her if I bumped into her.

"Oh I doubt you would have seen me," she dismissed, "there were so many people there and I was sitting in the studio."

"Sounds like you had a better view than Me," I said.

"I doubt that," she said almost laughing.

I was not sure why exactly she doubted it. My seat was quite an ordinary chair and there would be no need for Me to go into the studio itself. I think it is private anyway as this is where the theater performers change so I do not really feel that it is somewhere I should be going into. After all, I wouldn't like anybody in My locker room before a match.

"Were you tired at the end of it?" She asked quickly glancing at her notes.

"No, I would not say that I was tired at all. I was sad that it ended and would have been willing to sit through it all over again."

For some reason here she seemed really perplexed this time, "That really is quite something for you to say that. I do not mean to be rude but at your age most players begin to look at the options regarding retirement whereas you sound really pumped wanting to sit through it all over again! That is so great to hear."

"To be honest I don't think My age had anything to do with it, anybody can do what I did, the main thing is to make sure that you enjoy yourself otherwise there is no point in going," I tried to explain.

"I am not quite sure 'anybody' can do it quite like you but I guess I am seeing what makes you so humble. What did you do afterwards?"

"I felt really energised and had so much fun so I thought it would be nice to end the day going for a meal with some friends."

She looked confused again, "Some friends? I didn't know you were friends with Serena? That's great!"

"Serena? Sure we are friends and you can say we have been working together for many years, she is great!" Though I had no idea why she mentioned Serena. Maybe she was there too. It would have been fun to sit together.

The interview ended shortly afterwards and I stayed behind to sign some autographs for the television crew and their families. It was only in the car on the way back homes that a staff member pointed out that perhaps the interviewer was referring to the Wimbledon final and she did not know that I was talking about the lovely evening at the theater. You see the point I wish to make for you? We had a perfectly normal conversation yet were talking about very different things. So My advice is always be sure you and the person you are talking to are discussing the same subject. Then even when you are certain of this, remember that the meanings of the words you say will be interpreted by the receiver's head library, regardless of how many floors your own head library has so always be mindful of the misinterpretations.

Sometimes perception can be used to your advantage. Have you noticed that during some of My matches I occasionally play somebody who has been doing well for the entire tournament, then as soon as they walk out on court to play Me, suddenly they are unable to string two shots together, let alone string their racquet. Why do you think this is? There is nothing that I can do to cause them to do the chokings and hit the ball in illegal areas of the court. Well, this is where the psychologies I have implemented throughout My career come into play. Do you think that the reason I do not join other players when they have fun together playing video games or playing the fun soccer matches is because I am not invited? Well, it is partly that, but I use this to My advantage or as they saying goes, I have turned the tables on the situation. This situation of them all having fun and leaving Me out means that they hardly ever see Me. They do not have the opportunities to see Me as one of them and indeed I am not. When they do see Me it becomes a large occasion, and their brains are recognising that they are not playing their friend that they were at the party with the previous evening. In addition and especially at Wimbledon, I may walk on court with crisp white trousers and

PSEUDOFED

perhaps a little white army style jacket. Who is allowed to do that? They certainly are not. This is when the moment of the perceptions really creates itself, for them, they are playing somebody they should respect more than any other player. This is why I now totally endorse the notion that players should not show their personalities on court. They must remain quiet and behave accordingly. Who remembers the time when Johnathon McEnroe and James Connors used to play the tennis? They had no respect for their opponent! They actually believed they could win and this created a perception in their heads that I am not very fond of. If people have the belief that they can beat Me, that may happen so I am not in favour of allowing this sort of behaviour to creep back onto the court thank you very much.

Incidentally, if somebody does want to invite Me over to play some games I would really, really, really, like this. I am free most evenings after tea time.

10

MEDITATION

Spiritual GOAT Quote. Proverb Correction Edition:
"When faced with adversity, do not run and hide."
Incorrect, sometimes it is best to.

— PF xx

Now I shall help you with some words about the importance of making the relaxings. Having some Me time should be an important and necessary part of your daily activity and your life, much like going to the lavatory and doing the tinkles. You may think one is more important than the other and that is because it is. I would place tinkling a little higher on the list of important daily tasks than relaxings, however, both should be listed and carried out. You may be able to go on court and play a great match without relaxing beforehand but it is doubtful that you could walk on court and be there for two or three hours playing magnificently if you did not sprinkle beforehand. You would not be able to run properly for a start and then during the breaks all those drinks would make the situation worse. So rule number one, before playing tennis or before relaxing, visit the little GOAT's room and do the necessary things, not forgetting to wash your hands and feet afterwards.

One method of relaxing is meditation. I will be honest with you, I was never entirely sure what meditation was for a long time. I recall the first time that I first started researching on the interwebs about it and discovered that in order to mediate one needs a cushion. Not a nice plush cushion with your initials hand-sewn onto the corner but a rather small cushion. I ordered one of these some time ago and had it delivered at homes. When it arrived, I initially thought that they got the order wrong and sent a cushion for a hamster, then I opened the frustration free packaging and discovered this was apparently what I was to use for mediation. I looked at it for several moments searching for a zip where it could be undone expecting it to self-expand into something fifteen times its size, but no, it was this little seat and it was the appropriate size for the bottoms, apparently. I did not feel entirely convinced but I was prepared to give it a try.

The instructions also gave diagrams as to how one should be seated for the meditations. There was no mention in the booklet of getting staff to assist you in getting into such a position so I assume this must have been lost in translations. Nowadays they seem to use automatic online translators rather than real people and the essence of the original message is often lost. It is a little like the game Chinese Whispers though I am not sure if they play this game in China. Anyway, the instructions described how I should place the small cushion on the floor and sit on it. Then you are supposed to bend one leg quite far back underneath yourself so it creates almost a loop. Then with the other leg you thread it through the loop and out, lastly you hold onto each ankle and pull both legs tight. Apparently you are supposed to sit still like this for several hours. At the time I was not quite sure what was going to happen, I kept looking over My shoulders almost afraid of what to expect. Nothing did happen.

This led Me onto an interesting journey to find Myself. I do not mean that I did not know where I was, I always know that. What I am referring to here is being in search for truth. There is a difference between the truth and the knowledge. Knowledge is for the brain and gives you a false sense of the being. If you have read a lot of books and perhaps have the PhD or The Three Degrees, you may think you know lots of things but do you know the truth? Remember that there is a difference between believing and knowing. For example, what if you booked a ticket for a time travel trip and went forward one hundred years from now and looked back at all the knowledges you acquired today, would they still be valid? Even if some of them will, most will not. So whatever is it you think that you believe now will be replaced with something else in the future. Therefore it is not truth, truth does not change and is constant, otherwise it would not be called truth and would be called something else, like asparagus.

After making the realisations of this I decided that I should travel the world in search for the truth and discover the ancient art of the meditations as everybody told Me this would be the doorway to finding it. When I began the journey it was quite difficult to plan. For those of you that follow the tennis you will already know how full the tennis calendar is each year as I mentioned at the beginning of this beautiful book. It is difficult to get any time off, no matter how far in advance you submit your vacation slip to Mr. ATP. Usually we get some time off in December then it is a rush as all the players try to book their vacation times during the same metaphorical window. I have witnessed the little arguments in the locker rooms as they rush to book that last place in Disney World only to find that Ernests Gulbis had already booked it in advance, probably because he owns the hotel. Rumour has it that he has enough money in his piggy bank to buy more hotels than Paris Hilton, though to be fair I do not believe that she only has hotels in Paris.

Having borrowed a lot of books from a good friend of Mine, Janko Tipsarević, I discovered that the place I had to visit to learn about the meditations was Nepal, not to be confused with My former coach, The Paul (Anaconda). Nepal is where Mr. Buddha lived and he knew a thing or two about meditating. I do not actually think he wrote the book on it but he certainly contributed. So what better place to visit?

I thought such a journey would be quite lonely so I ordered Stanford Wawrinka to come with Me. At the time he had not yet won his first Grand Slam and was much more obedient than he is nowadays. Having said that, he still needed the occasional correction and I liked to use positive reinforcement using treats. An antidote I often tell at parties is the time I first knew he would make a career as a professional player and essentially discovered him. I was out taking him for a walk one day in a park, it was early in the morning in Switzerland (a country) when a tennis ball from nearby public courts got miss-hit and came out and into the field where we were walking. As soon as Stanford saw it he shot off so fast that he pulled the lead straight out of My hand. I had never seen such quick reactions and was pleasantly surprised! From that moment I knew he had a promising career and when I took him back home, I told his keeper that he should enroll Stanford into their local tennis club. The rest, as I say, is history. You're welcome.

When I told Stanford he was coming with Me to Nepal his first reaction was that he couldn't as he had made plans. I told him to shut up and start packing and an hour later we were on Fed Force One having just taken off. I untied him and gave him his packed lunch in a cute Tupperware container that had his name on the lid. Inside he was treated to a cheese and ketchup sandwich, a chocolate chip cookie and an apple. He looked at Me and asked what I was having, I slid the menu across the table for him to see but snatched it back quickly as he attempted to touch it. During My banquet I discussed the purpose of the trip with him and how I had always been curious about the meditations and what better place to go than Nepal to learn about it. He asked why I couldn't have just bought a book on the subject. That was a valid point and one I had not thought of.

We landed in a timely manner and I dismissed the cabin crew telling them that they were free to take in the local scenery but not stray too far from the airport in case I got bored and wanted go homes at short notice. The chauffeured car was waiting after going through the airport V.I.P. procedures. I climbed in the car acknowledging the driver holding the door open and put a little piece of chocolate in his pocket as a tip. He then got in the driver's seat, started the car and we were soon on our way to the hotel for the first night's stay. I looked back out of the car window as we pulled away from the airport and waved at Stanford as he was in line waiting for a taxi. There did not seem to be too many people in front of him which was encouraging as I did not cherish the thought of waiting for him at the hotel to check him in. My car journey was uneventful and I leaned forward looking out through the side window at this beautiful country. I remember wondering whether it was for sale but did not want to get sidetracked so made a note to add it to My Amazon Wish List.

Forty five minutes was how long I had to wait for Stanford at the hotel and to say it was a little irritating is a rather large understatement. I looked up as he ran in the hotel reception looking flustered and lost so I got up and gave him a little wave and gestured that we should approach the reception area to check-in. As we walked over to the front desk a member of the hotel staff noticed Me and recognised who I was which was nice and meant that I was greeted in an appropriate manner. The pleasant gentleman gave Me the key card to the Presidential Suite which I slipped into a pocket. He then confirmed Stanford's room as a King Size Executive suite with view of the mountains. Stanford looked pleased and eager. I interrupted and asked if they had a standard single room on the ground floor for him instead, which they confirmed was available. After the formalities the receptionist asked if I wanted a selection of newspapers and breakfast the following morning, I nodded in agreement.

Stanford immediately said, "Me too, thank you," but I raised a hand and shook My head.

I encouraged Stanford to accompany Me to My suite as I had a lot of bags. Upon entering the room he whistled in a manner that suggested it was impressive. I thought it was a little small. I told him to leave the bags there, took out My wallet and gave him a dollar. He took it although looked surprised for some reason. I told him I was going to turn in early as I had a bit of a headache after the flight.

He then started a barrage of questions, "Is it just a headache?"

"I suppose so."

"Do you feel any other symptoms?"

I was not sure where this was going with this line of questioning, "I do not know, even on My plane it is still a long flight, I just want to get a good night's sleep OK?"

He got a little more assertive, "If you think there is anything else wrong with you, you are obliged to tell Me."

"What are you talking about? I do not have to tell you anything," I said, almost raising My voice.

"Yes you do," he insisted. "Before taking any treatment I must be given full details."

His voice was getting louder and he was becoming increasing agitated so I eventually shooed him out really not having any idea what all that was about. I remember thinking that I hope this sort of behaviour does not show itself on court, say in a Grand Slam final in Australia.

I woke up early the next morning and filled My lungs with the lovely fresh air that was flowing through the suite. The weather outside looked inviting so I smiled to Myself, leaned over and pulled the hanging rope by the side of the bed. The butler came in, immaculately dressed, carrying a tray that had little legs so the tray could be placed across My lap. I observed that these legs did not have knees. As the butler approached

PSEUDOFED

I noticed that the tray was filled with a lovely selection of local foods. I pushed Myself up into a sitting position and rubbed My hands together in excitement. A little yelp escaped Me as breakfast was placed across My lap. I thanked the gentleman and asked him to leave. I do not like people watching Me as I eat. I enjoyed the delicious foods whilst quietly scanning the local newspapers that were open to one side. Once finished eating I sat on the side of the bed, slipped the feet in the plush slippers and went to have a shower. As I was drying My hair afterwards I thought I heard a sound. I was not sure of its location as I had the hair dryer on. I looked out of the window, there was a tree nearby so I imagined that it must have been a squirrel or something. As I was getting dressed I heard it again, it was a definite scratching sound except this time it was much louder and was coming from the double-doored entrance to the suite. I walked over and opened one of the doors just a little and saw that it was Stanford, I closed it again.

After getting dressed I left the suite and gestured to the butler's desk outside the door that I was going out so they should clean the room. As I walked down the steps I placed one hand on the banister as I was making the steps, the wood did not seem to be a soft grain and I considered talking to the front desk about this. Stanford was sitting on a couch in the foyer so I walked over to him.

"Bonjour," he said, "I thought we may have breakfast together, I got up early and found a great place just 10 minutes from here."

I told him I had already had breakfast and that we were going out now. He sprung up excitedly asking where we were going and I told him to organise a taxi and call Me when it arrives. He then ran outside following my command. After about five minutes he came back into the hotel and saw that I was sitting on the couch reading a magazine. He was making some strange facial expressions. I got out My portable telephone, found the Contacts page, swiped until I came across his name and tapped the Call icon.

I watched him signal to Me to hold on as he took his phone out, "Hello?" he said. He did not have My number so was not aware that it was Me that called.

"What is it?" I asked.

He looked at Me from across the large room, "Why are you calling me? The taxi is waiting."

I ended the call, got up and walked straight passed him and got into the back seat of the car. It was not the usual standard that I was accustomed to but remember feeling that it would suffice.

Stanford looked at Me through the open door, "Are you going to slide across so that I can get in?"

"No," I said with an expressionless face. It looked as though he rolled his eyes as he shut the door. As he walked around to the other side of the car I quickly slid across to that side. He opened the door, looked at Me and took a big sigh asking what I was playing at. I made the giggle faces and slid back allowing him to get in. He did not seem to find it funny and all in all was not in the best of moods for some reason. I told the driver to take us to where Mr. Buddha lived and we pulled away from the hotel. It would have been a pleasant journey other than Stanford continually asking if we were there yet.

We arrived at a picturesque small village. I got out of the car, thanked the driver and told Stanford to pay him. Looking around it was not obvious where Mr. Buddha lived.

"He actually did not live in a house," said Stanford. "Siddhartha Gautama, as was his original name, lived in a palace, son of a King, and left it all behind to learn about how to be truly happy. He meditated for years in a forest sitting under a tree and living very simply. When he achieved enlightenment he realised that each and every one of us already have everything we need to be happy. Today's materialistic and consumer based lifestyle is a distraction to us discovering who we really are." He went onto explain that a long walk up the side of a mountain from this village is the location of the Bodhi Tree where the Buddha meditated and obviously is now a major attraction to millions of people from around the world.

I looked at him for a few moments and told him to shut up. I led the way to a clearly signed and well worn path. The cool breeze was refreshing against the heat of the sun. After about five minutes Stanford said he needed the toilet. I told him he should have gone before we left the hotel and that he would have to wait.

After about three hours of walking we came across an isolated but absolutely stunning looking restaurant. We both stood outside and looked through the windows, it really did look inviting and made Me do the salivations. It was nearly lunchtime so it made sense to stop and rest before continuing. We went in and were promptly greeted by some pleasant restaurant staff. I smiled and said, "Table for one please." I told Stanford that I was going to eat here and that he should keep walking. I gave him My number so that he could send Me a text message when he arrived. He asked if he could at least use the toilet and I said he could but only if he was quick but then he had to go. I was led to a table by the window at the back of the restaurant that had a tremendous view from the side of the mountain and across the valleys. I was given a colourful menu which I could not read, what made it worse was that it did not have any pictures either. When the waiter arrived I told him My name hoping for a reaction but in return he just gave Me his name. I asked if he watched tennis and he said that he did not. I was not quite sure what to say next, it is not often I am in a position where people think I am ordinary. After a little pointing at what other people were eating we seemed to understand each other. What transpired was a lovely experience of one of the best meals of My life. With nobody recognising Me it felt like I was in disguise, almost invisible. It was a fun experience but not one I would like to have too often.

I ordered a coffee and some fruit for dessert and enjoyed the relaxation times. My portable telephone made the good vibrations.

It was a text message from Stanford, 'I am here, what do you want me to do now?'

I paused before replying, the possibilities seemed endless. My fingers tapped gracefully and with purpose, 'Look for the tree,' I then tapped Send without needing to check for errors.

After a few moments the reply alerted My phone into action, 'What does it look like?'

'It has a trunk with branches coming off in random directions from about half way up, it may have leaves on it too,' I replied quickly. It really was a stupid question.

After a couple of minutes he replied, 'They all look like that. Leave it to me, I have found a guide that has offered to help.'

I did not bother to reply, besides, I think sending text messages whilst abroad can be quite expensive. Although I must say, when you have homes in so many countries, what does the term 'abroad' actually mean? I pondered this question for nine minutes.

The dessert was lovely and tasted like the freshest fruit I had ever eaten. I checked the time and it was the middle of the afternoon. What was Stanford up to? If I walked up to join him it would be dark by the time we walked all the way down again. I really was keen to find out more about the meditations but did not want to be out at night in an unknown location. I left the restaurant and walked back down to the village where we were dropped off earlier. During the walk down the path I occasionally did some little sprintings which was fun. Still in great shape. I'm welcome.

At the village I noticed a bar with some taxis outside so I made a jaunt over to the first car and took a ride back to the hotel.

Upon entering I made the little wave to the friendly faces on the front desk, they certainly knew who I was. Walking up the stairs to the suite level I decided to take two steps at a time which was tiring. Once on the correct floor I skipped My way happily to the double doors of the suite and entered closing the door behind Me. The room had certainly been serviced and looked perfect. I quickly popped My head in the bathroom to check the flowers had been changed on the counter and smiled to Myself when I saw they had. I was not quite sure what to do next so decided to check out what was on the television. I was about to reach for the remote control when a cheeky thought asked permission to enter My mind to which I said, "Yes". I smiled at the idea that was now in the brain. I looked sideways at the bed, quickly took My shoes off and leapt on it jumping up and down as if it were a trampoline. I giggled to Myself, I had not done anything like this since last week.

The rest of the day and evening was fairly uneventful, I watched some shows, a movie and what seemed like a detective drama on the television. I then had dinner and told the butler that he was going to play Monopoly with Me. I won, on the basis that I owned all the properties before the game began. By eleven o'clock Stanford still was not back and I was wondering whether I should be worried. I decided not to think about it until the morning as it was quite late and so went to bed.

I woke up after a very restful sleep. I think I dreamt about owning an island but then realised that I probably already did so was not sure if it was a dream or just a memory. I turned to the beside clock which indicated that it was ten thirty, quite late. Switching on My phone I thought about Stanford again wondering if he had gotten back yet. There were not any messages from him so I decided to call for breakfast. Rather than the same food as the previous morning, for that day I had already pre-booked a nice big bowl of chocolate coated rice puff cereal and almond milk. I still enjoy it to this day as it turns the milk chocolaty.

After showering I ventured downstairs, My hair was still a little wet as I had not fully dried it but decided it looked quite good. Stanford was not anywhere to be seen. I gave a little wave and mouthed, "Hello" as I approached the front desk and asked the team if they had seem him or whether he had returned. They all looked at each other with uncertain faces but one of them said that he returned just a few moments ago and they thought that he was in his room. I thanked them and took Myself to the ground floor single room I had booked for him.

I knocked on the door and it opened with the pressure from the knocking, it had not been shut properly. I thought to Myself how stupid he was not to close it securely, did I have to think about everything for him?

Nonetheless I did hope he was OK. I walked in gingerly looking around to make sure I was not in danger from intruders. Everything looked normal. As I walked past the bathroom to the left and into the rest of the room there was Stanford, legs crossed in the Lotus position. I slapped him across the face asking what he was doing. He immediately opened his eyes and gave Me the biggest smile I had ever seen.

"Hi!" he said. He definitely did not look his usual self, why was he sitting like this? Where had he been all night? What did he have for breakfast?

"Don't you ever stay out that late again without telling Me!" I scolded.

For the next couple of hours he told Me what happened after he arrived at the location the previous day. He met a wise guide who taught him everything he knew about meditation and enlightenment. Stanford claims he sat there all night outside meditating and as the sun broke early in the morning he achieved enlightenment before returning back to the hotel.

"What does it actually mean?" I asked.

"It is like you see the world through different eyes," he explained.

I looked at his eyes and they certainly seemed to be the same ones that he has always had. I thought I had better check to be absolutely certain so I quickly pulled out My portable telephone, went to the browser and searched the interwebs for pictures of Stanford. I found a good one and with the fingers did the pinchings and the zoomings to focus in on one of his eyes. I held the phone by his face to compare and yes, they definitely were the same eyes.

"That guide, the man you saw, he's lying." I said. "Your eyes are the same as they were yesterday and here is the proof," I tried to explain pointing at the iris picture I had on My phone.

He smiled again, he did not seem to be bothered by anything. "No, that is not what I meant GOAT." He went on to explain that everything in the world is the way it is supposed to be and that attachment is the source of all suffering so ultimately we should learn about acceptance.

I thought for a moment and remembered how everybody regards Me as the greatest player of all time, I was starting to like what he was saying.

"We have to appreciate everything that we have in this very moment and also the fact that nothing ever stays the same. Everything changes," he continued.

"One day in the future another player will come along and be considered better than you and so it will continue, it is just the natural order of life, and that is the way it is supposed to be."

"How many more Grand Slams do I need to win so this does not happen?" I asked, irritated by what he just said.

"No, it is fine," he tried to reassure Me, "just enjoy it right now, in this moment."

I slapped him across the face again, "You are trying to tell Me other players from the future will be better than Me? There is nothing fine about that, get your things together, we are going home."

He calmly got up and gathered a few essential belongings saying he was leaving everything else. He said he now recognised the attachment he had to everyday things and materialism does not bring happiness.

"Look!" I said sternly, lifting My sleeve and pointing to My expensive timepiece. "Do you know how much this is worth?"

He looked at it, smiled and said, "Yes it certainly is lovely, but it is only a watch and one day it will cease to be. It is really quite meaningless in the grand scheme of things."

I really was not liking this new Stanford. "What if I did not have Fed Force One, how would you get home?" I said smugly.

Unperturbed he said, "I would just get a ticket and travel with other people on a scheduled flight, maybe I would arrive a day later, but what does that matter?"

Now he was really starting to sound ridiculous.

We traveled back that same day and all the way during the flight he was gazing out of the window seemingly amazed by the sights. I looked too but did not see anything worth smiling about. There were just fluffy white clouds, nothing exciting there. It was a good flight and upon landing I went back homes, not sure where Stanford went, I left him at the airport.

Looking back I do not really regret My negativity towards Stanford at the end of the trip, I did learn a lot and did not regret taking him along. He has never been the same since and I am not sure whether to be proud or feel responsible. I though, have since become a master at the meditation and in the following chapter I will gift you a special guided meditation which I know you will enjoy. I am still not sure about this enlightenment. Stanford seems so happy now when I see him and is always full of the satisfactions. I am not sure how anybody can be satisfied with what they have so if this is what enlightenment is, I will not be purchasing it anytime soon.

11

GUIDED MEDITATION

Spiritual GOAT Quote:
"I think I am great, therefore I am."

— PF xx

Following from the previous chapter I now offer you something very special, a guided meditation from Me to you. This is the first time such a valuable guide has been given to humanity as well as animalanity, so I encourage you to cherish this moment, it is history in the making. You can read it through once, twice or even more if you wish, then put it to good use and allow it to change your life forever. I recommend doing this meditation at least once a day. It is particularly useful before something stressful like a big tournament or match. For you perhaps before an interview for a little job or something. Although the two make the overlappings, meditation and relaxation are technically different and I shall discuss the latter in the following chapter, after this one, next. Two chapters from now it will be the previous chapter. Having said this, meditation can be considered a method of relaxation but it focuses on relaxing the memories inside the mind, which is inside the brain, not sure where.

Let us begin.

You should find a quiet room but to make the honestations this can be done in any location except the cinema due to the tempting smell of popcorn. With experience as you become more of an expert you will be able to do this almost anywhere and at any time, at homes or even on a yacht during a party times.

To start with and especially if it is your first time, expel the family and staff from your home. Tell them to go shopping and buy you something nice. This way you can do the meditations with the bonus of a lovely surprise when they return. Once they have gone, go to your favourite room and make sure it is not cold. If you feel the little chill in the air, use the touch screen room sensor by the door to adjust the climate to your desired setting. You want to be very comfortable so should wear loose clothing. If you are wearing shoes or similar footwear please remove. The same if you are wearing a silk scarf around the neck, please take it off.

I encourage you to keep socks on because toes should be covered at all times, they are small and can move on their own which can be most distracting.

Sit somewhere and ensure that it is quite comfortable, you do not have to maintain the Lotus position, any other flower will suffice, I like the buttercup. Allow your arms to rest down by your side and rest your hands on your knees using one knee for each hand which is rather convenient. Try and use the right hand for the right knee and place the left hand on your left knee, it is just easier this way.

Now you have the correct posture take a deep breath, relax both shoulders and close both of your eyes. I have tried with just one eye shut and it does not work as well so remember to do both. Now, breathe in through your left nostril, slow and steady. When your lungs and abdomen are full your tummy should stick out just a little. Now exhale slow and steady, but this time from your right nostril. After exhaling if you find that your tummy is still protruding perhaps you ought to think about a change of diet. Go back and read the relevant chapter now. Do not return to this chapter until you have put your tummy back in again.

As you do the breathing feel the air pass through the nose hairs freely and just enjoy the sensations, do not breathe too quickly or it may become itchy. When you have repeated this a few times the calm feeling will become normal. It is so normal for Me now I sometimes do not even realise that I am doing it. I do it sometimes during the press conferences and even during a match either when sitting down and the ball servants are holding the umbrella over Me to create the shade, or just before I am about to serve as I lean forward and gently touch the ground with the tip of the toe of My back foot as I bounce the ball.

The objective of this meditation is to learn the art of acceptance and letting go. I am not referring to the racquet by the way. I mean that letting go means to not allow yourself to be angry or frustrated. If you accept a situation, regardless of what it is, you cannot be upset. Remember, nothing can ever make you angry, it is your reaction to a situation that causes the anger, not the situation itself. Therefore, we are going to make the focus faces on acceptance. This works for any and every situation hence why I stress sometimes that I choose to lose matches. I never lose by accident, it is always a choice and one that I accept.

You will never be in a similar position to Me so you will have to scale down your visualisations. Something like accepting that you will probably only be able to see Me play on your small television set rather than being able to afford to buy a ticket and attend a tournament. I am a major star, a household name, somebody important.

You are not. Accept. You cannot change this even if you wanted to, so better to accept. Breathe deeply. Inhale.

Take a deep breath and repeat this mantra, 'I am nothing.' (Note, I am talking about you, not Me.)

Say it seventeen times and then exhale. You should repeat this daily until it is internalised and every cell in your body believes it. Again, it is truth whether you accept it or not, so better to make the realisations and the sooner the better. Obviously I have another mantra, several in fact. There is no point in sharing them with you as you are never ever going to need them. Accept. Exhale.

'I am nothing.' Breathe.

Now is the time to come out of the deep relaxations. Do this gently with no sudden movements otherwise you may do the hurtings. Firstly start to re-engage your mind away from mantras and the calm state of affairs. Think about the normal mundane things in life. For Me it is something like choosing whether to buy or build another homes. You will be thinking about other things that I could not possibly imagine and I do not want to try either. As your body returns to its normal state you will feel more relaxed, calm and content. Look around and smile, be happy with what you have, it is unlikely to ever be more than it is now, actually it will likely be even less in the future.

From this exercise we can see the benefits of doing the meditations. You can feel relaxed and refreshed. But it is not all about this. You can also meditate on problems you may be facing in your lives. This means rather than making the mind go silent, you only think about one issue and freely allow every thought to enter offering possible solutions. Let Me make the examples.

During *that* Wimbledon final of 2008 I was doing a lot of the meditations because I was the big fan of the television series, Lost. What was the polar bear doing on a tropical island and what was the black smokes? Like many people I was trying to work out these puzzles and took it upon Myself to resolve them. We had rainy delays during the match so there was little else to do. Unfortunately for you, I was not on the Twitter technology making the tweetings back then. Rain delays can be irritating at the best of times but they are also a good excuse to lock yourself in a room you know that the BBC Television presenter, Sue Barker, cannot reach you. I think the gentlemen's locker rooms are the one place she does not have access to. I hope that does not change in the future due to laws of the opportunities that are equal. Anyway, at the time I wanted to focus on the Lost numbers:

    4, 8, 15, 16, 23, 42.

What better times than the rain breaks to meditate deeply on the hidden meaning. If Jack did not know, I knew it was up to me. I do not think Mr. Hurley was capable and Sawyer seemed too busy making the flirtatious faces with somebody he called Freckles.

As I sat on the bench in the locker room during the first rain delay I felt happy with the way I was playing. Roland Garros that was only a short time before was now just a distant nightmare. I watched carefully as staff removed My socks for the massaging of the calf muscles. As they rubbed coconut oil in My skin I closed My eyes and thought about Desmond. What was he doing in the hatch? Who told him to put those numbers in the computer? My mind wandered back to the final I was in the middle of playing, I felt calm and relaxed how the match was going. How long had Desmond *really* been in the hatch?

My fiancée came into the dressing room and, as you probably read about at the time, it seemed her sole purpose was to tell me what My name was. I looked at her making the ponderings. I already knew My name. When I was a little GOAT at school My mother would sew My name onto My clothes. Now I am older every item of clothing I wear has My initials on them, even the undergarments. So why did she want to remind Me of My name at such a crucial time in a match? Talk about stating the obvious. I did not really have time to question her further so I thanked her and gave her a signed photo.

Closing My eyes again I remembered the match. I had not chosen to lose, not at that moment anyway. As I stepped onto the court after the first rain delay you will remember that I appeared to be totally aware and compos mentis, well at least compos, maybe not so much the mentis. Yet the reality is that I was deep in advanced meditation. Advanced? Yes, I was using both sides of My brain independently of each other. With the left side I was making the contemplations on the most efficient way to win the third set, with the right side I was trying to decide whether Ben Linus was dangerous or really trustworthy.

It turned out that I did not win the following set as efficiently as I anticipated. But upon the reflection, it only delayed the inevitables. Ben seemed entirely credible when they initially found him. Staff and I wanted to believe that he was geniune, yet there was something about him that made Me make the wary faces and I am just not sure what it was. A little like one or two journalists I have encountered.

Before I knew it the spots of rain were falling again. Breathe. I accepted the situation. The match was not over and nor would it be until I decided. I rushed over to My seats, carefully folded My trousers and cardigan. I would have put it in one of My bags but I already had a jacket there with the number 6 embroidered on it in the anticipations. As I strolled back to the locker room I looked up into the sky. I felt good and looked good.

Once inside I heard voices of officials and staff. I think they were talking. Their lips moved but I could not hear what they were saying. Staff were hurriedly touching My legs doing a quick lymph massage. My thighs and knees were getting rather sore and I was worried they may do the crampings. My mind was totally in the present moment. I had to win the remaining sets in order to win the Championship. It is really all that needed to be done, nothing more and nothing less.

"OK GOAT, you are good to go. Go and get the job done, Champ!" a staff member said. I was surprised at how quickly those 30 minutes passed. I did not resist the situation, I allowed it to be.

Once out I quickly got back into the game. Accepting, breathing, always wary of Ben Linus. I decided Jack should not trust him. It was getting dark and I could faintly hear the commentators' raised voices as the match was nearing its conclusion. I did not have to think about the game at all. Another advantage of advanced meditations is that you can engage your body into autopilots. It had been a good flight, it always is when you have a private jet. But now it was time to descend and prepare for landing.

We got up after a pleasant refreshments break and Rafaello was leading 8-7 in the fifth set and was serving. He indicated that he had new balls and I politely acknowledged him, thankful it was quite dark so nobody could see My blushings. The rally started with his first serve which was good. I was relaxed, eyes almost closed and letting My body breathe for itself. I was grateful for everything I had, especially the things that money can buy. Rafaello's shot went long, proof that no effort was required on My part and also evidence that it did not matter whether his balls were new or partly worn. Fifteen Love. Exhale and accept.

The next point was served wide, I closed My eyes as the ball approached and effortlessly moved through the air for a fantastic return. Rafaello was already approaching the net and quickly hit, what some people may call, a winner. I was unperturbed as I looked at his biceps. Glancing over to My box I thought I noticed they were all looking at his arms too. Distracted, nobody seemed to notice that it was his first serve and volley that he made in the entire match. For him to resort to this meant that I had obviously backed him into a corner. Time to make My move? I felt comfortable, so much so that I seriously considered whether I should form the Crane Kick position that Daniel LaRusso famously used in the 1984 documentary, The Karate Kid. His mentor, Mr. Miyagi suggested that this move had no defence. Was it fair to do this to Rafaello? I know the tennis rule book inside and the out and I can make the confirmations that it does not mention that The Crane Kick is not allowed. I inhaled and focused on the ground beneath My feet.

Subconsciously the mind had decided that as soon as the press conferences finished, regardless of the winner, I should try and get Jack's number and warn him about Ben. Maybe I could send him the SMS text message or perhaps just call? I knew that once you enter the Wimbledon grounds there is a time shift and you are transported to 1936 and this is true to this day, however, I was not sure how that effected the time difference to the Lost island.

It was 'advantage' to Rafaello on his serve. My body had won points during this game. This illustrates the power of meditation. You can simply carry on with your lifely duties and yet your mind is in the deep trance. I took a deep breath, closed My eyes and heard the loud roar of the crowd. I snapped the eyelids open and saw My opponent on the ground, he looked in pain. I was not sure if I was allowed on his side of the court during a match, and anyway, if there was a problem it is better to leave it to the professionals. I sauntered over to My seats and sat down. The match may have been over but My career was far from it.

Checking My things I noticed the jacket with "6" still sealed hidden in one of the bags. I thought it best not to take it out and wear it. I smiled to Myself thinking, "There's always next year."

There appeared to be lots of celebrations going on around Me. Have you ever been in a room full of people yet somehow felt totally alone? I haven't. I knew that My subconscious choosing to lose the match was the right and selfless thing to do. The fans had been watching for hours. How fair would it be to not finish the final that night? I know that if it was Me watching a match I would be given access to the Royal Box, but for normal people like you this is not, or ever will be, an option. Accept, breathe.

Inside I was content and calm. Why exert energy unnecessarily? While Rafaello was climbing up to his family and walking across the roof tops to make the celebrations, everybody was in some sort of mass hysteria appreciating Me because I chose to end the match early for them. But Me? I was calm, relaxed with a steady pulse of 56 bpm and blood pressure of 120/60.

Start meditating today, you never know when you are going to need it.

12

RELAXATION TECHNIQUES

> Spiritual GOAT Quote Correction Edition:
> "A Problem Shared is a Problem Halved"
> Incorrect: A Problem Shared is a Problem Doubled.
>
> — PF xx

The previous two chapters explained and helped you understand and carry out the meditations. This is essential to life and something you should take seriously. So many times we let others' opinions control our lives and many of us have lost our inner strength without realising that this is something we should never have given away to begin with. We must find it again and take it back now.

PSEUDOFED

Earlier in this classic manuscript I spoke about the importance of having Me time. Not everything is about serious meditations or other rituals that you have to carry out with perfection. Sometimes you just want to have fun doing the things you like to do. As the great Cyndi Lauper once said, GOATs just want to have fun.

So what can we do for the relaxings? Well, My life is different to yours in a way that you will never be able to imagine and that goes for Me too, or as they used to say in Ancient Rome, 'vice versa'. Therefore, I have no idea what sort of help I can offer you, however, all I can do is tell you what I do and perhaps from that you can pick up some ideas.

Something I have done for many years is write poetry. It is very personal for Me and something I have never shared until now. I know you will revel in the marvel that awaits. You're welcome.

> The GOAT the GOAT they call My name,
> To not please them would be such a shame.
> I'm rarely at homes due to My job,
> My Dad's name is Bob.
>
> Grass is nice because it's green,
> When it's with blue it should never be seen,

I glide along, barely sweating,
Which cuts the cost of the deodorant
I'm getting.

The commentators hail Me as their hero,
For breakfast I like more than one Cheerio,
They say that I am so sublime,
I ask Chef to give Me a twist of lime.

Wherever I go the fans always support,
Even the French prefer Me over their chocolate torte,
As they shout vous êtes le meilleur,
I smile and say mes voitures ont des moteurs.

Can it be true that I am so great?
I knew it was, from the age of eight,
I wake each morning with a smile on My face,
My favourite type of rally starts and ends with an ace.

My FedBerry will not leave My hand, not even after a grapple,
People often ask, 'Majesty, why don't you have an Apple?
I smile at them as I sit on My boat,

> And reply, 'That is for sheep, I am the GOAT'.
>
> Mr. Bradlings' words often make us think,
> Using his twitter account he often tells Me to have a drink,
> He works for ESPN and also owns a tennis store,
> Mr. Bradlings, Mr. Bradlings, you always leave us wanting more.
>
> Thank you Dear Diary, this story is at its end,
> I will go now, staff will put down My pen.
> Feeling relaxed after writing another gem,
> Everything I do is a classic, I can count to ten.

It will surprise you to learn that I wrote this in a very short amount of time. I know you appreciate My revealing something very personal here. I am keeping My poetry that I have written over the years and perhaps will publish it for the world one day. I am certain that Harvard, Eton and other schools would do all they can do get their educated hands on the first editions.

You should try and do something like this too and I really encourage that. The world today is so fast and quick, we often forget the beauty of just being together with friends or just alone, sitting in a rather large field perhaps and just enjoying the nature. Poetry can merge all this together. Do not be discouraged when you first start writing. True creation is something that cannot be taught, look at Me, nobody taught Me anything, I merely am. As you can see My poetry is of a classic style, at the very least equal to the works of John Keats, Jane Austen, William Shakespeare or Justin Bieber.

For you it will take time but do not let this deter you. I know we often hear the phrase that Practise Makes Perfect but this is not true. Perfection is not made, it just is. For you, the action itself of continually trying will just help you relax and enjoy some self time. Do not worry about the words that come out, just write. Let us face the truth together, it is not as though you are going to be famous and publish your works. But that is OK. It does not mean you cannot relax. You certainly can and you have every right to. Frankie did.

I really want to stress about the importance of relaxing but really, perhaps we need to understand what it really means. Many confuse relaxing with having the fun times. Watching a movie or dancing to some great music is actually not making the relaxings. These things are distractions. They are often confused with relaxing as it gives people a change from something that is mundane. Distracting is not relaxing even though they rhyme. Relaxing is not sleeping either. Sleeping is something different and involves keeping your eyes closed for often long periods of time. Relaxing, on the other hand, can perhaps be described as doing nothing. Not meditating, but just spending time with yourself, making the contemplations on life, what you have achieved and what you want to achieve. Even perhaps wondering how you can help others and maybe improve their lives. If you are relaxing in the nature times, perhaps a small squirrel will join you. Do not make any sudden movements, just watch the little squirrel fan and make some soothing noises as if to say, "Hello". You may have a few hazelnuts in your (white) jacket pocket that you can offer to your new little friend. These things are relaxing. If you have a doggy fan as a pet you can go for long walks in your many acres of land. You see, these are just some ideas on how to relax and My expert advice is to give this equal importance to things like meditation and improving your self-awareness.

Having said all this, I do not wish to take anything away from having fun, especially with friends and staff. Having fun is a big part of relaxing if done correctly. I place a lot of importance on this and am about to reveal something that, until now, has been off the record. For those that are not familiar with this term, 'off the record' is an oath journalists make to keep the secrets.

For example, if I say 'hello' to Mr. Ben Rothenberg, he is free to write about it in the New York Times. However, if I say, 'This is off the record, Hello Mr. Ben' then he is sworn not to tell anybody what I said.

What nobody has known about until now is that some of the guys and Me sometimes get together and have a lot of fun creating music. You may know that in the history of tennis some players have been in bands. Patrick Cash plays the guitar, so does John McEnroe and yes, I am being serious. The Bryan Brothers are also in a band although they look suspiciously similar. Personally I think it is one person creating the optical illusions just to confuse the opponents, nonetheless there appear to be two of them and they make the music as well as the tennis.

Have you noticed though that there has been a media black-out on today's players and their music antics? Yes, until now it has been a secret. But with kind permission of most of those involved I can do the revealings of the band, The Tennis Rackets!

This started not long ago after another major. I was watching a music channel on the television set after a stretch on the mat. I had recently chosen to go out of the French Open in Paris (France) and was feeling good about My game. The show on the television was featuring boy bands and the concept looked fun.

I do not play any instrument apart from the Wilson so thought it would be fun times if I got some of the others together and we could form a band like those on the show I had been watching. As it was My idea I decided that I would be the Capitano which meant I could choose who was in it and who was not. Staff made some calls.

After a moment the FedBerry started to make the good vibrations. This was how the first call went:

> Me: "Hello."
> Caller: "Hi Rog it's Tim."
> Me: "Who is this?"
> Caller: "Henman Rog, Tim Henman."
> Me: "How did you get My number?"
> Caller: "I heard you're setting up a band and thought it was a great idea. When can I come over?"
> Me: "Sorry, wrong number."

Shortly after, the phone started to vibrate again:

> Me: "Yes, GOAT speaking."
> Caller: "Hello GOAT, it's Tomas."

At this point I suddenly remembered that it had been rumoured that Tomas Berdych liked to have naked photographs taken of himself and was considering doing more for sponsors. Something we now know to be true.

> Me: "Tom, what are you wearing?"
> Tom: "Jeans and a t-shirt, why are you asking? Anyway, can I be in the band?"
> Me: "Yes, but it is not a stripper thing, we will be keeping our clothes on."
> Tom: "Oh really? That is a big shame but let us catch up later so we can discuss it."

I took a few calls and in no time at all we had a great looking band. There was Me, Tomas, Maria, Andrew and Fabio (Fognini, not Lanzoni, unfortunately).

Stanford wanted to join in too but I dismissed him. Ernests Gulbis also showed some interest but said he would only join if there were not any females in the band. Well, even though I originally intended it to be a boy band, Maria said she would give Me a free packet of Sugarpova if she could be in too. I agreed on the assertion that it was a bag of Sporty Mix. Ernests was therefore, out. Not because Maria was a band member, but because he made such a request to begin with. I told him that his space was taken by a girl just to annoy him.

The first meeting and rehearsals went well, given the circumstances. Tomas arrived wearing a rather large coat and whispered to me to guess what he was wearing underneath it, followed by a cheeky wink. I thought for a moment and suggested it was a shirt with a rather pleasant neck-tie, and a fashionable pair of Bermuda trousers. He laughed and said I was very wrong so I ignored him and welcomed Maria.

She screeched into the dance hall and everybody covered their ears, I had staff cover Mine. Andrew smirked his way in and asked who was in charge. I lifted My arm and said I was. For a moment I thought he rolled his eyes. Next entered Fabio, swaggering in also wearing a big coat similar to that of Tom's. He looked very pleased with himself as he stood next to the bird man. I thought the dress style that him and Tom were wearing was a little unusual to say the least. Just big overcoats? Certainly not the height of fashion, more at the lower end of the scale. What was I wearing I hear you ask? I had some freshly pressed trousers, a lovely ruffled shirt and a scarf.

Before we started Fabio walked up to Me in a very strange, slow but confident manner of walking, I remember thinking to myself at the time. He placed his hand on My chest and said, "Ciao Bello!". I was a little taken aback but thanked him for the compliment. He smiled and did not move, his hand still on My chest. I looked down only to discover that he was holding a pocket mirror and had been looking at himself the entire time. I still thought that I looked nice.

I walked into the middle of the dance floor and announced that I would show them some moves that they should follow. I glanced back at a staff member who knew to press the play button on the portable disc player and the music started to thump and then I made the groovy faces as I felt a rather stylish choreography routine coming on, a little like how I play on court. First by just moving the head from side to side, then the arms in outward rotations and it finished with a sprint to the left and throwing both arms forward.

Andrew clapped and said, "That was Gold, you should be awarded a medal."

I was not impressed with what he was trying to say and as I told him so, I noticed that he was trying not to laugh. I raised my voice a little and exclaimed that such insubordination will not be tolerated.

Maria actually did very well in following My moves. When it ended she let out a scream again which echoed around the room and one of the windows shattered. This was quite alarming so I arranged for everything to be cleared up before we continued. Remember kids, safety first.

Next was Fabio and Tom who said they would dance together. It looked very strange as they danced in these full length coats. When they ended the routine, they grabbed their coats and when their arms went out, so the coats opened. I screamed loudly, a little like Maria's on court screech but Mine was in a different key. I then ran out of the room as fast as I could. I can confirm that Tom was not wearing what I originally guessed. I am not sure what either of them were wearing, it is all such a blur yet I know for sure that I do not have one in My wardrobe.

After a few moments I went back in only to find the team practising the dance. I skipped in amongst them and joined in the fun times. I giggled as I made the moves, we all did. If only the press could see us now. I asked Tom and Fabio to keep their coats on.

We met a few times after that to rehearse our show and I must say we worked really well. If I had to say somebody did not pull their weight properly, I will say that it was Andrew. He just seemed to be there to gain material to make up jokes about Me. I let him stay because I always treat others how I wish staff to treat Me. He was not grateful with the opportunities I have granted to him, never has been.

Next up was us having to decide a name for our band. We had a meeting about it over lunch one day.

I wanted us to meet in a restaurant in Switzerland. It is one of My favourite places not far from homes. The chef there knows Me and I always get the extra scoop of ice creams for dessert. I do not even charge them extra for this when I send them the invoice for the pleasure of My eating there. They're welcome.

Despite My sending everybody a SMS text message from My wireless portable telephone advising of the GPS co-ordinates for the restaurant, Fabio immediately replied to the group saying he wanted us to meet in his favourite pizza restaurant that was actually his house in Italy. When everybody said yes to his idea I felt a little like the odd GOAT out so for the interests of the democracy I agreed too.

When we arrived at his house later that week Fabio opened the door and greeted us saying, "Benvenuto". I told him that I did not speak Spanish and asked him to stick with English for the sake of everybody else. I remember looking around as we walked into the house and thinking that it was relatively pleasing to the eye. Though I must say I found the transparent plastic covers on the sofa and chairs a little odd. Tomas caught Me looking and whispered that it is an Italian thing. We were offered a little aperitif by some of Fabio's family which was very tasty. I raised My hand and asked where the little GOAT's room was as I needed to make a tweet. Fabio personally led Me to his personal bathroom and kindly offered to stand outside the door in case I needed anything. I was a little startled upon entering as the walls and ceiling were all mirrored. I must say though that other than this it was quite beautiful with the biggest bathtub I had ever seen. After I finished doing some business I washed the hands carefully and then rinsed well. As I was drying them it was even more startling to see that the floor was mirrored too. Lucky I noticed this now and not a few minutes before.

Walking back with Fabio I asked him why his bathroom had mirrors everywhere. He smiled and gave Me a wink with his left eye, then he made a strange clucking sound with his mouth and said, "You can never have too much of a good thing eh?". I told him that the noise he just did made Me feel uncomfortable as I was a GOAT, not a horse. He slapped Me on the bottoms and said, "OK GOAT". I know he is always a little forward but perhaps this was a little inappropriate. I asked Tom about it later who again said it was an Italian thing.

By the time we all sat to eat I was getting quite hungry. Fabio sat at the head of the table, I allowed this as it was his house. I sat at the other end. Andrew and Maria were to My right and Tom was on the left. The meal consisted of delicious Italian favourites like macaroni, stuffed artichokes, farinata and of course, the pizza. On the table there was a generous selection of grissini breadsticks which, to this day, I am certain that Andrew kept stealing Mine. Why did I have to sit near him anyway?

I announced to the table the name I chose for the band, The Tennis Rackets. I wanted something original and fun. Tom suggested The Slice Boys but I said that was too obvious. Andrew suggested The Shank Boys but immediately retracted it muttering something about if we call it that it would only have one band member. I am not sure what he was referring to but am quite certain that it was related to Me, it usually is. Fabio rubbed his chin and suggested we call it, Fabio's Boys. Maria screeched loudly and said, "Hello?"

"Hello Maria fan," I replied politely.

She then made a point that we could not call the band 'Boys' because she was a girl. Everybody looked at Me. This felt like a player council meeting but a little more serious. I took a cork from a wine bottle and using a match I set fire to one end. I let the cork burn for just a few seconds until it turned black then I blew it out in a single graceful puff. Everybody's gaze firmly fixated on Me, as usual. I let the cork cool down then I stood up and walked over to Maria. I gestured that she should be still. Then with the black burnt end of the cork I drew a moustache under her nose. Fabio clapped,

"Bravo Bravo!" I casually walked back to the chair and sat down feeling good that I had just illustrated to everybody how to be positive and take action when faced with problems. I looked at Maria, smiled as I poured Myself some water and asked her what she thought.

"Pseudo, this does not make me a boy, it is just a stupid moustache drawn on with a burnt cork!" she said.

Talk about being ungrateful. Always being one and a half steps ahead of everybody else I said that it looked quite good. Maria screeched again and My glass cracked. She said that it does not matter how good it may or may or may not look, she was a girl and not a boy. I wondered for a moment in silence trying to think of what else we could do to make her a boy then posed the question to the table. Andrew laughed, seemingly at Me and said that Maria was a girl and for me to stop being so stupid. I tried to kick him under the table but missed and hurt My other foot.

Of course, Maria was indeed correct and if everyone had listened to Me to begin with, we would not have been having this discussion. I reminded everybody that I was the boss and the band is not going to be called anything 'boys' and we are going to be called, The Tennis Rackets.

Andrew wanted confirmations about the spelling of 'rackets' and after I advised him he said that he was surprised that I was smart enough to think of the double meaning. I told him to shut up.

Tom asked if we should all be given names as band members. I told him we already had names decided by our Mummies and Daddies shortly after we were born. Andrew laughed again and said that is not what Tom meant. I raised My hand and told him to stop being so disrespectful and that I was a legend of the game of tennis and to the world and under no circumstances was he to talk to me like that again.

Fabio stood up and announced, "Signore e Signori, vi presento, Humble Racket!"

I quickly stood up too and told him to stop speaking in that funny language and he cannot be Humble Racket as I wanted that name. A little argument ensued in which we agreed that neither of us would use this in the name of fairness. In order to keep this process moving as efficiently as possible I said that everybody could advise of the band name that they would like for themselves but the final decision would be down to Me. I agreed that this was the best way forward.

Tom reached into his pocket and had a handful of photographs that he dealt out, almost as if we were playing cards and he was the dealer. Fabio got his photo first, he raised his eyebrows and said, "Grande!" I was curious. Maria looked at the photo, raised her eyebrows and grunted. Why was I the last to get Mine? Andrew grabbed the picture that was dealt to him and said, "Respect". Finally I got the photo everybody else had seen, all the photos that he shared out were the same. It was a picture of Tom, naked. I quickly covered it up and asked Tom what was the meaning of this? He said that he wanted to be known as 'Naked Racket'. I looked at the photo again. He certainly did have a point. I agreed.

I looked at Fabio and advised that he would be called Italian Racket. Andrew muttered that that was too obvious and that I may as well call Fabio, Spaghetti Racket. I wanted to reply something witty that would put him in his place but could not think of anything. I ignored him and looked at Fabio to see what he thought of My band name for him. He nodded and made an interesting gesture with his hand so I assume he was accepting My notion.

Maria said she did not mind what she was called as long as it was not something like, Screechy Racket. I took a moment to make some contemplations and decided that she should be called, Confectionary Racket. She thought about it and nodded in agreement. Andrew again had something to say. He said it was long winded and not catchy at all. I told him to shut up especially as it was his turn next. I was tempted to name him, Annoying Racket but I did not want to appear rude, not this time anyway. Andrew would be called, Stealing Racket.

"What does that even mean?" he asked.

"You stole My Olympic Gold Medal," I told him, as if he needed reminding.

"I didn't steal it," he said laughing. "How could I steal it? I just beat you."

"You did not beat Me, I chose to lose," I said defiantly nodding to Myself in agreement.

"Why do you always go on about choosing to lose? You're no different to anybody else, you just lose,"

I stood up quickly and said I had never been insulted like that in the whole of My life, nor the life before that. I asked if he knew who I was. He did look a little startled at My reaction and said defensively that I was a tennis player like everybody else on the tour. I could not believe the level of insults that he was throwing at Me. I paused for a moment, sat down and thought about the band. This was about all of us, not just Me. He is young, I thought to Myself, I inwardly forgave him.

Everybody was named in the band other than Me. I wanted to save the best until last.

"Do you have any suggestions about what I will be called?" I asked everybody.

Tom shrugged his shoulders. Fabio said Chocolate Racket because if I was a bar of chocolate I would eat Myself. I ignored him as I did not know what he meant. I looked at Maria, she stood and and walked to the corner of the room and turned her back on all of us. After a few seconds she came back to her seat and said that she had not thought of anything. I reluctantly looked at Andrew.

"Old Racket?" he suggested as everybody laughed.

I actually did not think this was a bad idea and was not sure why everybody was doing the laughings. Somehow it did not have a certain ring to it but I took it onboard and it helped Me make a decision on what I wanted My name to be in the band.

'Elder Racket.' As in: Wise, looked up to, leader, suave, sophisticated and a little bit old fashioned.

Despite the usual sarcastic comments from Andrew of the Murrays, which I was more than used to, every agreed and so the band was born. Looking back it really was a pleasant day. During stressful moments I just kept reminding Myself that I was doing this for fun and relaxation and this helped a lot. We thanked Fabio for his hospitality and left.

We did several rehearsals behind closed doors. Naked Racket eventually succumbed to My request of at least wearing something, albeit a baseball cap. It was off putting at first but you just get used to it. Once we felt comfortable with our routine we took the show on the road. We performed our show in private after several tournaments to the other players and a few selected journalists and commentators. If you are reading this and it is news to you, your invite did not get lost in the mail.

You see, even with all the energy involved, it was true fun times. This should not be compared like programmes on the television set, watching the electronic box is something I seriously do not recommend, unless I am on it, in which case it is a top recommendation. Rather than look for shows, turn it off and go outside and do something, perhaps with some friends. Maybe you will start a band too like I did. These kinds of things get you so involved in something that is fun and at the same time you are making the physical activities, which is far better than just sitting watching a screen. Spending fun times with The Tennis Racket band was a great experience, even with Andrew, at times anyway. What we did was fun and it is something I recommend you do from time to time with your friends, if you have any.

13

DREAMS

Spiritual GOAT Quote. Proverb
Correction Edition:
"You know what they say don't you?"
No, actually I don't.

— PF xx

Gabrielle says that dreams can come true. But what is a dream? We must make the definitions before we know if they come true.

A dream? You probably have the ideas already about what one is but you will allow Me to make some definitions on your behalf. 'Some' definitions you wonder? Yes, because, of course there is more than one type of dream.

We should start with making the obvious faces and talk about the night-time dreams. You make the dreams at night when you think you are sleeping. But yet you do not sleep, you never sleep. You may be confused at this point because what I am writing is very advanced. You see a new and further definition is needed before we an move forward with this discussion.

When I say 'you', who or what am I making the references to? Or rather, where? If you have a mediocre memory you will realise that we have touched on this before in a previous chapter. That is the notion of the self. Who are you? How are you? I am very well thank you. Where are you? No, not your location in your small apartment, but *you*. Do you exist in a particular part of your body? Your foot perhaps? A leg? No, so where do you exist, your brain? If you are your brain you would not refer to it as *your* brain as though it is a possession. You cannot be something that belongs to you. Do you see what we have revealed? You refer to every part of your body as though it is property and we have quickly discovered that this property cannot be you, therefore, *you* cannot go to sleep. Your body goes to sleep and this is when we have night-time dreams. But you? You are always awake watching the dreams.

Further discussion into the location of where your self resides is beyond the objectives of this book and probably too advanced for you anyway. My only point here was to make the highlightations that such discussions should not be approached lightly, or slightly.

To make the conclusions, you can see that night-time dreams which was the first definition that I wanted to discuss, are more than just little stories that your brain has created. These are little stories of fantasy, a goal or aspiration such as perhaps meeting Me, or even maybe being Me. Now you must be dreaming! They are ways in which your brain is telling you that you must do better in your life. A sort of unachievable goal, a lot like having a staff member dangle a carrot in front of your nose whilst you go for a walk.

But what about Me and My dreams? Would it be so silly if I dreamt of being Me? Well, of course not. I am an icon, a legend, the very being and aspiration that you to look up to. You are welcome. Seeing as I have no aspirations or goals, as I am these notions in their very essence, My dreams will be different to yours. I dream of fashion styles and fun colours to wear in the Spring. Sometimes I dream about being the greatest tennis player of all time, though this is more of an autobiographical documentary full of facts rather than a typical dream that often does not make much sense.

Night-time dreams are often categorised as good or bad. Bad dreams are called nightmares and are are often when someone or something is chasing you. A mystical creature that has large ears and a small nose, it thunders making the ground shake with each leap. You keep running, your heart pounding as you run for your life but it seems that no matter how fast you run, it is still catching up. As it makes that final leap you scream and wake up in the cold sweat perhaps making the shoutings. It may surprise you to learn that I occasionally have nightmares too, well, two actually. Yes. Let me recount them for you. They are very easy to remember as they are both recurring.

First is the repetitive short dream. The first time it happened I thought it was an abduction by aliens. I was lying in one of My beds, smiling to Myself as I was slowly drifting off into the sleep. Suddenly a very bright light shone on Me. My initial reaction was to smile, wave and thank everybody for their support, yet there was no cheering. Then I felt Myself being transported very quickly, it happened so fastly that it was almost instantaneous. Suddenly I was lying on something resembling a gurney in an operating room. I tried to look around but felt paralysed. This made Me very fearful. If these were aliens then there was a very slim chance that they had never heard of Me. Somebody not knowing who I am is a nightmare in itself so you can imagine how desperate this situation was for Me. At first I assumed that it was the guys from the ATP wanting a sample but usually they give Me a little cup and run

PSEUDOFED

the tap to help Me. But this was not like that, they were taking blood. Is this what happens when a urine sample tests positive? I was just terrified. I then realised it was not the tennis officials. I think what gave it away was the grey complexion and the pointy ears. The fact that they were about 2 feet and 6 inches tall I think was what really convinced Me beyond doubt. As I struggled and fought with all My might to escape this situation I woke up screaming. I quickly sat up, looked out of the window at the beautiful tropical view from My homes (you'll have to use your imagination) and I was back. I sighed the big relief and realised that it was nothing but a dream yet it was already time to get up. As I laid back down I thought to Myself, "It's OK GOAT, why don't you cuddle in for another 15 minutes?" I immediately replied, "Yes please, thank you."

The second dream is a little longer and actually worse in many ways, even if it may not seem that way. I have this dream nearly every night so will refer to it in the present tense as this is how it feels. It starts off as I just arrive at a familiar location ready for the next tournament. During the press conferences I speak about how great My chances are of winning, all the tournament staff and fans are all so pleased to see Me and scream My name. I give them a little wave and for the few lucky ones, perhaps sign the autograph, all pretty standard. Then I get the complimentary transport back to My luxury accommodations. A staff member opens the door as I approach, I acknowledge them and thought I heard them reply, "de nada" as I walked past. Did I just hear that correctly? No, I brush it off as doing the mis-hearings. I stroll into the kitchen looking for Chef. He looks different to normal yet somehow familiar. His hair is longer and arms bigger. As usual I make the assumptions that he has everything under control for My supper so I go into the dining room to await My din-dins. I choose a space at the table and make Myself comfortable. As always the table is prepared and everything is just how I like it. Yet something is not quite right. All the water bottles on the table have their labels facing in the same direction. That is odd. Must be a coincidence. Chef eventually walks in but rather than walking straight towards Me, he seems to follow some imaginary lines on the floor, his feet occasionally double-stepping. He sits beside Me, his legs jittering very quickly. I look at him wondering why he hasn't brought in My alphabet shaped pasta on toast, a personal favourite of mine. He finds a towel and starts drying himself. It feels like I am waiting and waiting. The fur on the back on My neck starts to stand up, something isn't right. He pulls out a small sachet and puts one end in his mouth whilst squeezing the other end with his hands trying to force its contents out. I begin to feel unwell. I talk to him, asking what he is doing but he ignores Me, making Me wait. I look around and see thousands of people all watching. Why isn't anybody saying anything? Where is My dinner? He eventually leaps in the air and suddenly I get a cold feeling. He looks at Me, eyes piercing, and says, "Buena suerte".

I scream, unsure if I am actually dreaming. Faintly in the background I can hear commentators talking about how graceful and sublime I am and really the result is irrelevant as in their eyes I will always be the GOAT. I feel a sense of relief but I can still see Chef leaping up and down before Me. Why is he sweating so much? He gives Me a glance and tells Me to follow him into the kitchen. I don't want to. Where is My alphabet pasta? I have fun collecting the, Gs, Os, As and Ts and eating them last. I enter the kitchen and he tells Me that he's going to prepare a nice dish of pasta.

"Alphabet pasta?" I ask. My voice sounding feeble. This is not the Chef I hired is it? From behind Me a bendy looking gentleman appears. His hair is quite dark, thick and almost black. I am tempted to touch it.

"Gluten free pasta?" he shouts.

Chef seems to laugh a little. The water is boiling ready for the spaghetti. He shows Me how he adds some salt then says, "Olive oil, of course. Just a little in the water, Extra Virgin."

I scold him for being rude. Again he laughs as he lowers the pasta into the pot. The oil didn't look familiar. Usually I like a particular Italian brand so I asked him where is My usual oil.

"This is better," he says, "Spanish".

I become weak and feel as though I am turning fifty shades of grey. Meanwhile the man with the nice hair is dancing around the kitchen. He points towards Me with his index finger and tells me that, "This is you."

What is Me? Then he swaggers around the kitchen and with every third step he flicks his hair back. He then leaps as though he is ballet dancing. For a moment I thought it looked familiar, stylish and quite pleasing. Chef was watching, laughing. There was nothing funny about it. They giggle together, sharing some sort of inside Djoke. I just don't like this situation. Where are the rest of My staff? I poke My head out of the door looking up one of the hallways. I double-clap My hands which is how I usually let the team know that I am in need of something. Instead of the quick shuffling of feet that I normally hear as they try to get to Me as quickly as possible, I don't hear anything. Only the two strangers in My kitchen. I feel sick.

The pasta is ready and both of these guys prepare it for Me, it does actually look quite nice. The one with the thick short hair escorts Me back to the dining room and tells Me to get comfortable. He refers to Me as, 'Your Majesty' and says My food will be arriving shortly. Maybe this isn't a dream after all?

Chef eventually walks out of the kitchen and waves goodbye, "Hasta luego," he yells as he runs out. Why didn't *he* bring Me the meal? Surely he doesn't expect me to fetch it Myself? Where was the other bendy looking one? Out of the kitchen walks a very smartly dressed waiter carrying a feast fit for a GOAT. This is more like it. The plate had one of those dome shaped covers on it, I usually insist on these anyway so felt reassured.

As he lays the dish before Me he asks if I am ready for the good stuff. "This will put hairs on your chest," he says. He had an accent, 'Was it Scottish?' I asked Myself as he lifted the dome and I saw what looked like a rather large baked potato on the plate.

"Where did you ever find such a potato?" I asked.

He smiles and tells me that it is a Haggis.

"Haggis? I normally have the King Edward variety." I explain.

"It isn't a potato you fool, it's Haggis," again laughing at Me. He was somewhat impolite to say the least.

"What is in it?" I asked, a student of worldly cuisine that I am. But he leaves without answering.

Unperturbed I begin to eat. Certainly an usual texture and a little more chewy than I expected. He was right, this wasn't a potato, I certainly wouldn't want to mash it with butter let alone make fries out of it. By the end of the meal I wipe the corners of My mouth with a plush napkin. I'm about to leave when I hear the sound of a trolly from the west wing coming to where I am. "Hello?" I called.

"Hello GOAT," another Scottish accent but this time a lady. She was pushing a trolley full of desserts. Delicious! She winked which made Me do the blushings. As she walked around the trolley towards Me she did some wiggles and asked if I wanted to do the Salsa. I made the perplexion faces and said that I couldn't see any nachos and that I was actually hoping for a little cake.

"Not that kind of salsa, silly GOAT. How about some Cha Cha?"

"Bless you," I said and offered her a tissue.

Behind Me, there was a loud crash and there he was, standing before Me again, that Chef. I looked back and the nice lady had vanished. It was just Me and him, again. I had that sick feeling just as when I initially walked in. Everything always goes so well in My life but then he turns up.

"No, go away!" I exclaimed.

I feel an ever increasing tightness in My toes and I continue screaming, yelling and bleating. I flail My arms around wildly trying to push the world away, when will it ever stop, why is it always him?

Suddenly I am awake, I am covered in the sweat. I look at the bedside clock and it reads 3:33am. I sit on the side of the bed relieved that it was all just a dream but disturbed that I suffer it so often. I look towards the corner of the bedroom and gesture to a ball boy to bring the towel. After drying off I get back into bed, grab the spare pillow to cuddle, and fall into a peaceful sleep.

So, now we have discussed the first definition people usually think of when they think of a dream. I think it is fair to say that we have all experienced nighttime dreams in our life times.

From a scientific perspective dreaming is an integral part of sleeping. The type of dreaming that happens when you are asleep can only happen when, you are asleep. Scientists have discovered that sleep has different stages and you cannot achieve the later stages without going through the first steps. For example, one of the advanced stages of sleep is often referred to as, R.E.M.. For those of you unfamiliar with this term it means, Rapid Ear Movement. This happens during the dreaming state. To an onlooker, if they look very closely and if your hair is short enough, they would be able to see your ears moving quickly, almost flapping. It is all quite fascinating really. I have asked staff several times if they can record Me sleeping so I can see Mine in action but unfortunately we have not yet been able to record this phenomenon due to My night head band covering the ears thus preventing the seeings.

So what other type of dreaming is there? Yes, you are correct. Daytime dreaming. Something you do quite often I imagine. What is daytime dreaming and how does it compare to night-time dreaming? Well first we need to make the divisions. If you fall asleep during the day and dream, is this daytime dreaming or night-time dreaming? Obviously the daytime is not the same as the night-time otherwise how would we know when to go to bed and when to get up? However, does your body know? No, your body is asleep so for all the very tense and purposes, it is night-time dreaming regardless of when you sleep. This concept can be difficult for the average person, such as you, to grasp. To make it easier just think of your eyes. You shut them when you sleep and when you shut your eyes everything goes dark. Darkness only happens at night. So you see, this is an easy way to distinguish that when you sleep, no matter what time of day or night it is, it is the same as night-time sleeping because your eyes are shut, therefore it is night, even if it is day. I hope that makes it more clear for you.

Daytime dreaming is when your eyes are open and therefore you are not asleep. This can actually happen during the night too but I am not getting into that again. Your eyes are open and you are definitely awake as you cannot be asleep and awake at the same time. Picture this, you are awake in your badly air conditioned office, your mind may drift off as you wish for something better. I can certainly appreciate this although I have no idea what it feels like. You are likely to imagine Me, a mentor for so many. You make the visualisations of Me walking out on court, probably Wimbledon, fans making the cheerings, everybody from the small children to the senior fans with a smile on their little faces. You see My crisp white trousers, perhaps a lovely plush cardigan or even a little jacket with lots of pockets. The commentators so excited to see the GOAT tells you, Mr and Mrs Viewer, how happy you are to see Me. You feel elated, you sense what it is like to be Me although you would be wrong, it is far better than you could begin to imagine.

You have lost yourself in these thoughts, I imagine a little smile is now on your face and you do not even realise it. Then your boss person bangs on your desk asking why you are not working. You make the startled faces. You are brought back to reality and the images of Me that filled your senses a moment ago are already a distant memory.

What I have just described is daytime dreaming. It is something we all do, yes, even Me. It may surprise you very much to learn that unlike the night-time dreaming, My daytime dreams are not so different to yours in that even though I would not rather be anybody else, I do also think of Me. I smile to Myself appreciating all that I have achieved and all that I am. There is no boss to bring Me out of this state because I am the boss, in a different way to Bruce Springsteen, but we are both bosses in our own way.

I use daytime dreaming to help Me during the career. I still wish for things. Yes, it is true, even Me. I often daytime dream of how My life would have been if one or two tennis player had chosen a different career path. Allow Me to use a simple list with perhaps little personal notes to indicate how much My career would have been different if the following individuals had not been in tennis. For the sake of fairness, I will choose players totally at random:

> Rafaello Nadal - My career? A lot different.
> John Lloyd - My career? Not much different.

You see how this works? I can make the daydreams to see the path My career could have taken had certain circumstances or individuals had chosen a different career for themselves. For Me, greatness and fashion was My destiny so that was never going to be in question, the only difference is to what degree do I choose the level of such great accolades. You're welcome.

So now can you use these amazing tools Mother Nature has given us to your advantage? Night-time dreams are different to daytime dreams. Studies have shown that during a night-time dream we have far less control over what happens during the story. Certainly there are no daytime dream horrors, we do not say, "Oh I had a terrible daymare, please cuddle Me." Night-time dreams often reflect how you are feeling. Perhaps it can be during that day or generally at that moment in time. Do these types of dreams release tension and make you feel better? No they do not. In addition, if you had a nightmare you would probably feel worse. So what is their purpose? According to Revolutionary Theory, first discussed by Mr. Charles Darwinian, everything that we have and that we are is because there is a revolutionary advantage of having kept it. For example, as we all know elephants used to have very small trunks then as the trees got further away they had to grow longer trunks and this is the basis of Darwinian Theory. Therefore, according to Charlie, there must be a reason why we night-time dream, it must be to our survival advantage. How? I do not know.

Daytime dreams, however, clearly help us in the life. They help you (you, specifically) escape from your daily life and wonder what it could be like to be Me. It it like having rest during a very long race because you are tired and you cannot see the finishing line. You wonder why you even entered the race, you look to blame someone but then you realise everybody else has also stopped and feels the same as you. It feels hopeless because it is. Do you have to go to work on Monday? Yes you do. Why are you doing it? To save money so you can one day buy a ticket to see Me play. Suddenly the race has purpose, you feel the energy and the springs in your steps. Whilst everybody around you still have the delirious faces you suddenly feel something deep inside, you run, your strides now giant leaps. You've never felt this way before. You are even thinking of working the overtime. Your heart is no longer suffering, it is pounding with joy helping you to the victory line. You call My name, "GOAT, GOAT, I love you GOAT." Keep running.

14

GOODBYE

"I am My sunshine, My only sunshine,
I make Me happy, when staff are grey."

— (Original written by Davis & Mitchell,
Since improved upon by PF. You're welcome)

This is the moment I know you have been dreading, the last chapter in probably the most important book ever written since Harry Potty. Please, take a second to make the pausations. Stop in this moment and as you take the air into the lungs, I would be pleased if you also exhale. As you do, exude gratitude as you accept that the masterpiece you are holding is the literacy version of machines that slice bread so we do not have to, or in My case, staff. Do not be sad, I am here for you. We can make the electronic communications via the internets and it will feel like I am with you by your side. Of course, the reality is that I am not anywhere near you, I do not even know who you are and it is extremely doubtful that this will change. If I am not on the tennis court I am either in a luxury hotel or at homes, not that the two are worlds apart, just saying.

What this chapter aims to do is help you come to terms (and conditions) with this book coming to an end. I will give you as many tips and ideas to assist your conversion back from the dizzy heights of My life and back far down to your life. I guarantee that you will feel better if you take the advice I give. Although I use the word guarantee, you will not get your money back if you do not feel the benefits.

In addition to the advice, I will also let you in to what it is like to be Me. You will learn more personal insights as to My likes, dislikes and generally know more about who I really am off the court.

This book is full of wisdom and I urge you to use it along with the techniques you have read in previous chapters in order to apply them in to your life. It does not matter that you do not play tennis. They can be applied to all walks of the life. Stay happy and healthy because in doing so you can enjoy My game until I decide to make the retirement faces. Perhaps you are reading this and I have already retired? What a terrible shame, for you. Although none of this matters. Of course, I spoke about tennis towards the early part of this book, given My career and how good I am it is difficult to avoid the subject. However, it is still a manual of life that will help you in your developments to be a stronger person. I am not only referring to the physical strength with the building of the muscles and tendons, I am also referring to the mental strength as well. Take in everything I have written for you and you will have an inner core of strength strong enough to sit on as though it were a chair.

I would like to take this opportunity to make the reflections.

When this book first developed in My head as a thought I remember being excited. I tried to make the imaginations about how you, My fan, would feel upon first learning that your master and mentor has written down something for you. Obviously this exercise was all but impossible for Me. How on earth was I supposed to put Myself in your inexpensive shoes? Well, it is not as though I did not try, I owed it to each and every one of you to do the very best I could. I remember standing in front of one of the mirrors I have at homes and just staring in wonder at the person before Me, this in itself turned out to be something I actually do each and every day.

The first time I tried this I was trying to imagine that I was you and the reflectioninations in the mirror was Me and that Me in the mirror was going to write a book and in it give Me, well you, wise wisdom. After about forty five minutes of finally getting everything the right way around as to who was you and who was Me I had a fleeting glimpse of what it may be like for you. It lasted for just a moment, like the blink of the eye. The thought was so exciting that I ran to the bathroom as I had to do the tinklings.

Within a very short time I shared the idea with My family and a small group of friends and staff. The news that the GOAT was going to write a book spread rapidly around the echelon of society that I occasionally mix with. If you do not know what the word echelon means, you are not in that group so do not worry yourself nor give it another thought. Within days I began to receive letters from fans who are regarded, in some circles, as achievers themselves. I shall share a small selection here for your enjoyment.

> From: Ms Britney Spears
> Hello GOAT,

A close friend of mine just left me a voice mail saying that You are going to write a book! I couldn't believe it! I was so shocked that I had to call her right back and ask her to tell me one more time.

I had better go but just wanted to drop You this note to say that I wish You the very best of luck, You won't need it, nothing You do goes toxic. When it gets published be sure to send me a copy.

> You were born to make people happy,
> Much love,
> Britney X

My reply:
Dear Ms Spears,

> Thank you for your undated letter.

> I appreciate your warm wishes and support. Do I know you?

Much love,
PF xx

☙

From: Leonardo da Vinci,
Carissimo PF,

> Ciao and come stai? I have been hearing around the village that You are thinking of writing a book! What a gift to the world it will be.

All is well here, I have been doodling with some sketches, crazy ideas like machines that fly and things. I've decided to take up a spot of painting too though I doubt that it will amount to anything.

Anyway, take care and I'll be sure to buy a copy of the book when it comes out!

Distinti saluti,
Leonardo

My Reply:
Hello Leonardo,

Long time no hear. I must admit I was more than a little surprised to receive a letter from you. What have you been up to recently? How long have you been learning Italian?

I have been meaning to call you about Kate to offer My commiserations, who would have thought that she would end up marrying Prince William? After Titanic I thought that you and her were going to marry. Do keep up with your sketches, the one you did of Kate was really marvellous albeit a little revealing. Still, marrying into a Royal family is her loss not yours. You'll always have the memory of what you both got up to in the car below deck.

Next time I pop to the Hollywood I will have staff call your people and perhaps we can do lunch?
Hugs,
PF xx

☙

From: Randy Ray Um
Dear GOAT,

So, Mum tells me that You're going to write a book? I sighed. Can't You just leave it? Isn't tennis and all the adoration enough? Now on top of everything else it'll be all about how great PF's book is.

FYI I don't want a signed copy or any copy for that matter.
Sincerely,
Randy Ray Um.

My reply:
Dear Randy Ray Um,

I'm not sure if we know each other, yet your name seems somewhat familiar, as is your tone.

Rest assured that you will not be receiving a signed copy, you will have to buy it like everybody else.

Please send My best wishes to your lovely Mother,
PF xx

From: Buzz Lightyear
Dear PF,

I have received a message whilst preparing for another intergalactic emergency. The message said that You are thinking of writing a book to share your wisdom with us. As I travel to infinity and beyond, I see us partnering to secure the future for all things living. Future generations will look back on us

PSEUDOFED

with gratitude and this is something we must accept with grace and honor.

I will probably read the digital version as I'll be among the stars when Your scripture is published so will have My team send it to me in space.

Your humble friend,
Buzz

My reply:
Dear Mr. Lightyear,

Having been a fan of yours for some time I was excited to receive your letter!

Can you put Me in touch with anyone regarding doing an exhibition match on another planet? I've broken all the records down here so am looking to do something that has never been done before. My only concerns are the travel arrangements and accommodation. Is it true that it takes a long time to go from one planet to another? Our calendar is quite full so if I substituted, for example, playing in Cincinnati for a one-off match in another star system, would I be back in time for the US Open? Can you recommend any good hotels? I've looked on TripAdvisor but cannot seem to find anything.

Always your fan,
PF xx

It is always nice to receive letters from friends. In this digital age of the gadgets and portable telephones along with the fast pace of life and My first and second serve, I do fear for the true art of letter writing. Keeping very old and out-of-date traditions alive and well is so important, after all, Mr. Wimbledon has made a career out of it.

So, what sort of things can you do knowing there is little left to read in this book? Do not fear, the GOAT is here. Next are the amazing ideas I was referring to that are sure to make you feel better in this last chapter.

When we talk about the book ending, this is just the semantic faces. A book cannot end in the same way that it cannot begin. A book is just a collection of words on sheets of paper or on a screen. You still have the book and you will notice that it looks the same now as it did when you first acquired it. The best thing to do when you read the last word is to go back to the very beginning and start to enjoy it all over again. And guess what? You can do this repeatedly forever and ever. Nobody will ever stop you from doing this. I can sense the joy rising up as this dawns on you. Smile, because it is true.

Starting a series of scrap books is also a wonderful idea. With the world now being so digital and everything being on the computer, not only are we losing the creativity of writing letters but also the fun of making tangible creations! Yes, collect together as many magazines and newspapers as you can that contain pictures and articles about the GOAT and cut them out. At this point I insist on making the emphasis faces and advise caution with using scissors or any sharp tool. There is a danger you may cut yourself so either ask a grown up (or taller) person to do this for you or wear very thick gloves. Why do you need to cut the pictures out? Well, if you do not and merely tear the entire page out for your scrapbook, it will likely contain pictures of other people. Who wants other people being in a collection of things about Me? I certainly do not. Dirty.

While you have been arranging your scrapbooks you will have surely come across your favourite photograph of Mine truly. Why not go to your local picture store and have this photograph framed with a frame, preferably around the edges. You can then take it home and place it on the wall (you could get one for each room? Just a thought) or even stand it on a piece of furniture that has photos of your family. Place My photo proudly in the middle. I have actually done this Myself by the way. Talk to the photo throughout the day as though I am actually with you, you never know, it may answer back. It has happened to me on more than one occasion. I was a little shocked at first until I realised that it is quite normal.

Should you live in a place where it is difficult to find a photograph of Me do not worry. Although I must say that if you said to Me that this was the case I would seriously doubt whether you are making the truthful faces. Where in this world can one not find a pleasant image of the GOAT? But OK, let us cover all the bases as our American friends say. We shall assume this to be true even though I am making the giggle faces at the thought of this preposterous idea. What else are your options? As the saying goes, Easy Peasy Make the Lemons and Do the Squeezy. In such a situation you go to your nearest sculpture workshop and take classes on how to create a beautiful replica of Me using some kind of stone or even marble (preferably the latter). These things take effort to create but they can last for a very long time so are worth the effort. If you travel to Rome in Italy they have lots of statues there so do use this as a guide to help get yourself started. Although I would like to point out that I have seen many Roman statues and usually they are naked with everything showing, even Mr. Sniffles.

You will notice I have made the references to letter writing, scrapbooks and now sculptures. The theme here is important as I feel that these are things that nobody is doing now. I do appreciate we must always move forward and change is good but I am concerned we are leaving important things behind. Let us not. Together we can start a revolution to keep alive old skills and traditions. I will continue to inspire you with My wardrobe.

Another tip for you is art. It is often said that I am art and I am only able to agree. You can buy some crayons or if you have some extra money perhaps even purchase some paint with a professional set of brushes and of course a canvas. Take all of these to a lovely field, enjoy the nature and breathe in the air and let your inner creativity flow. Picture My face in your mind and connect with Mummy Earth and see what happens as you paint. You will discover that paintings are not at all like photographs, they are often much more blurry and do not really look like the person they are supposed to portray, however, this is the point. Great paintings are all about the artist's interpretation of what they see or feel. Though please bear in mind that once you have finished your painting, if I look more like a cartoon character with big ears and a fluffy nose rather than a beautiful specimen of a GOAT that I am, then please set fire to it immediately. Again, please do so carefully and always use safety matches, goggles and a harness at all times.

In the evening whilst preparing for a lovely meal why not set a space for Me at the head of your table? You can use the framed photograph and place it by the plate. As you are stirring the sauce you can occasionally look over at the picture eagerly waiting for its dinner and share a joke with Me or tell Me about your hard day at work. I like to hear about how you people live so it will be wonderful to experience. Please note, I do not like cabbage as it gives a funny feeling in My tummy, I think that perhaps I am intolerant to it. In any case if you are making sauerkraut as part of the meal please do not put any on the plate for Me. I would like to also suggest that before serving the food that you remove the photograph of Me and place it back on the mantelpiece. It just would not be right if I had a splattering of food upon My face.

Perhaps a less obvious thing to do would be to go to your nation's capital and acquire the relevant documentation so that you can legally change your name to that of Mine. You will then hear My name every day as people talk to you. Please though do not be confused, you are not Me and I am certainly not you.

If you are too shy to change your name or think that your family are not ready for that quite yet, you can use the Twitter to make the tweetings. Why not create a parody of Me and make the funny messages for the world to see? I give you this tip along with everything else with pleasure and joy in My heart. Though I would like to be honest and say that I am not a large fan of these parody accounts.

Should all else fail, at least you should keep up with My sponsorship garments and such. You will be pleased to know that the team I have around Me work hard so that no sooner you buy a beautiful shirt, it will already be out of date so you will have to buy another. The last thing anybody wants to be wearing is things that are not in the latest trend. If this is beyond your financial reach, another option is to just wear clothes from about nine decades ago, I often adopt such a look Myself, much to Mr. Wimbledon's pleasure.

As time passes and more and more people buy this book and the surge continues to grow, do not be surprised if you see it in famous book clubs. The world famous chatting show host Oprah Winnipeg has a book club and no doubt she will be including this amongst her selection. I have always admired Oprah, she is a nice lady.

From there you will likely see it as a New York Times Bestseller. Everywhere you look I will be there. Even if you shut your eyes you will see My face looking back at you. Bookshops around this earth will stock it although they face a serious problem, which section should they place it in? Classics is the first thing that comes to mind but it would not be out of place in Self Help, Autobiographies, Spirituality, Cooking and of course if it goes anywhere, it certainly has a home in the Family section, under Husbandry.

As we draw to a close I think it is only correct that I share with you a little more of Me. Something that will allow you to sneak the peek behind the superstar you see on the screens and on the court of the tennis. What am I really like behind closed big and heavy wooden doors? To make this as exciting as possible I have collated the most frequently asked questions that I am asked by fans and it will be your pleasure as you read these, along with My humble answers.

Question: Is it true that your pyjamas are ironed so well that you could slice a tomato along the trouser crease?
Answer: Yes.

PSEUDOFED

Question: What would you have been if you had not chosen tennis as a career?
Answer: A helicopter.

Question: Rocky or Rambo?
Answer: Adrian

Question: What do you do to relax?
Answer: Sit or lie down.

Question: What is your favourite fruit?
Answer: Toffee apples.

Question: Do you have any hobbies?
Answer: Tennis.

Question: What is 23 x 56 - 211 x 931 /4?
Answer: They are all numbers.

Question: Which country do you most enjoy visiting?
Answer: Countries are human constructs, I am not human, I see the world as one. We are all one.

Question: Do you own a computer?
Answer: Yes but due to My busy life I do not get to go out in it as often as I would like to.

Question: What is your party trick?
Answer: I can make tennis players using balloons.

Question: How many vehicles do you own?
Answer: I am not a number, I am a GOAT.

Question: If you could give one message to your fans, what would it be?
Answer: Hello.

I know that you have enjoyed reading this probably more than I enjoyed writing it. Please do not get Me wrong, giving back to you in the form of these words has been one of My many achievements along with countless others. And to think I wrote it whilst still playing a full time successful career makes the mind do the bogglings. But no matter how much pleasure I gained from the experience, I imagine it will not be close to the thrill you had in reading it and for this, I sincerely thank you.

Much love always,
PF xx

GLOSSARY

Spiritual GOAT Quote.
Proverb Correction Edition:
"If you pay peanuts you get monkeys."
Incorrect, I have tried this with staff.

— PF xx

Obviously it is difficult not to talk about tennis legends without talking about Me. In an effort to remain humble I will not talk about Myself here. Instead I will introduce you to some individuals of our tennis times. I will also mention some current players that you should look out for. In addition to players I will include other significant members of the tennis family, none of them are related to Me or My family. This is by no means a complete list of everybody, if it were then it would be longer than a very long book.

Andrew Agassi: Not related to Andrew of the Murrays. He used to have long hair, then he had no hair, then he had long hair again. It's actually quite complicated and I recommend you read his book for details, I don't want to get involved.

Sue Barker: To some extent, her tennis career in the 1970s paralleled Mine in that to-date she won the French Open as many times as I have. After she retired from the sport she got a job at the BBC to talk about Me.

Marion Bartoli: Interesting serve. Champion, currently retired.

Boris Becker: Former top tennis player and champion. Does the coachings. Dresses well. Speaks German.

Tomas Berdych: Tennis player, often photographed naked. I have a special relationship with Tom on the Twitter interwebs. We like to discuss music trivia, especially 80s. He taught Me the true meaning of bromance.

Bjorn Borg: Used to be a very serious player. Now makes fun underwear that are a little too cosy.

Carole Bouchard: Skilled journalist and all round lovely person. May hire her as H.R. Director one day.

Mr. Bradlings: Changed his name from Brad Gilbert. Likes nicknames and is a walking encyclopedia of all statistics on every conceivable subject. Do not, I repeat, do not sit next to him on a long flight unless you're planning to write a thesis on sports.

Bryan Brothers: So good they named them twice.

Darren Cahill: Tennis commentator with several sense of humours. Used to be in Neighbours.

Prince Charles, Prince of Wales: A Prince. Member of a well known family. Does not like ugly architecture. Talks to plants.

Caroline Cheese: Top tennis journalist. Apparently if she cuts herself she bleeds sport, I have never seen this before. Please be careful Caroline.

James Connors: James is also known as Jimmy. Him and John McEnroe don't talk to each other.

Juan Martin Del Potro: Has too many names, very tall and one of the nicest guys on tour. Juan loves Bruce Springsteen so was Born to Run.

Novak Djokovic: I notice that he is very bendy and flexible. Published a successful cookery book which is not something one often says about tennis players.

Jo Durie: Player, coach and talks about tennis. I am one of her fans and, as you know, I don't say that lightly.

Roy Emerson: Roy is one of the few people who won all the slams at least twice. Something I have decided not to pursue at the time of writing. He went onto form the successful music band Emerson, Lake and Palmer. Lake and Palmer didn't really get into tennis, which is a shame.

Chris Evert: Another legend of our time. Tennis is lucky to have Chris and Chris is lucky to be able to talk about Me.

David Ferrer: Has more stamina than everybody on tour put together. When he's not playing tennis he stars in Game of Thrones playing, 'Jaime Lannister'.

Chris Fowler: One of the best dressed tennis presenters on tour.

Mrs G: Less commonly known as Kim. Married to Mr. Bradlings. Used to work in the United Nations.

Steffi Graf: I don't want to talk about how many titles she has but I was one of many who enjoyed watching her play. She went on to develop a special relationship with Andrew Agassi.

Tim Henman: British, ex Wimbledon specialist. Now a trainee Manager there. Well spoken and rather pleasant at times.

Lleyton Hewitt: Australian. Always plays entertaining, fighting and consistent tennis Home & Away.

Goran Ivanisevic: Former Wimbledon Champion. Everybody loves Goran and I do too.

Billy Jean King: Legend. Go and read about her and all she achieved along with the other top players. Do it now. Her last name is often the same word people use when referring to Me.

Robbie Koenig: Tennis Commentator that I like very much. Really likes the '80s though not as much as Tomas Berdych.

Rod Laver: Rod is still on tour today and is another player that did quite well. His nickname is Rocket although I don't think he ever went to the moon nor did he ever work for NASA, although I can't confirm either.

David Law: Not actually a lawyer but a radio presenter. Very tall and very nice.

Ivan Lentils: Former champion. Extremely serious coach. Don't tell him a joke.

Nick Lester: One of My favourite commentators along with Robbie Koenig (subject to change). At the time of writing Nick works with Robbie and Robbie works with Nick.

Feliciano Lopez: Quite handsome. Please see Judy of the Murrays for details.

Nick McCarvel: Sports writer that writes about sports. Once wrote a piece about Me in the New York Times so is therefore an Honorary staff member.

John McEnroe: Mr. McEnroe is probably best known for his outspoken faces but he was rather good on court too. John played in a time when tennis players were allowed to have a personality. Nowadays it is considered inappropriate to take your personality on tour and we are encouraged to leave it at homes.

Patrick McEnroe: Top commentator and former tennis player who has the same last name as John which is quite a coincidence.

Ed McGrogan: Online editor for Tennis.com. Very pleasant gentleman. May hire him soon.

Carlos Moyá: Owns the box set of Breaking Bad and likes to be called, Heisenberg.

Andrew of the Murrays: Took My Olympic Gold medal. Thief. To date still not prosecuted.

Jamie of the Murrays: Doubles specialist. Just as well, I don't need another Murray taking My Olympic medals.

Judy of the Murrays: Judy does not currently play professional tennis but she knows a thing or two about what makes an exceedingly good cake. Captain of My Fed Cup and top coach.

Rafaello Nadal: Apparently when he was younger he had to make a choice of whether to play football or tennis. To this day I don't know why I was not on his advisory committee. Why didn't you choose football? You should have chosen football. Please go and play football.

Dave Nagel: Top ESPN Media Relations person. Likes Me a lot, I have never met him but may choose to one day.

David Nalbandian: Great career and even better karate champion. He really does not like line judges.

Martina Navratilova: Achieved 18 Grand Slam singles titles and all in all more titles in tennis than staff have made Me hot dinners. As well as singles Martina was in Doubles and at the Olympics. At this moment in time as I type this for you, looking out of My window, I have only 17 slams but by the time I retire I may have chosen to exceed this. I've played in the Olympics too.

Courtney Nguyen: Freelance tennis writer and has a very pleasant writing style. We exchanged smiles once as I was waiting for an elevator that she just came out of, little did she know she was in the presence of the GOAT (true story.)

Mark Petchey: Top Broadcaster with sense of humour and should be the head of tennis (after Me).

Craig O'Shannessy: Tennis statistics expert who can tell you every percentage you need to know. He has confirmed I am 100% GOAT.

Caro Paquin: Very pleasant tennis blogger that speaks languages. Used to be called Carol.

Andrew Rodrickson: Fast server, sweaty baseball cap. Also appeared in the cooking show called American Pie playing the character, 'Stifler'. Sadly retired from tennis. Come back Andrew, we miss you.

Ken Rosewall: Another rock in the foundation that is tennis. Won every Grand Slam at least twice but I still like him.

Ben Rothenberg: Tennis writer for the New York Times and other publications. Very nice person and we share similar hairstyles. Has been trying to score a personal interview with Me for some time and probably will continue to do so.

Peter Sampras: Often referred to as 'Pistol'. Has a lot of hair on his person. The only player that could play basketball whilst actually playing tennis.

Kim Sears: One of Team Murray's special advisors. Before Kim met Andrew she used to be a language instructor teaching sailors' vocab.

Maria Sugarpova: Candy maker and often has problems with her volume control on court.

Esther Vergeer: If I'm not going to talk about how many titles Steffi achieved, I'm definitely not going to discuss Esther's achievements. Am I making the jealous faces? A little. She is definitely the GOAT.

Stanford Wawrinka: Australian Open Champion, 2013. Swiss. My partner in crime. Top person and an inspiration. I like him but not as much as he likes Me.

Serena Williams: I love Serena, she doesn't love line judges either. Serena picks up Grand Slam titles as often as I hire staff members.

Venus Williams: Venus and Serena are sisters and together have won more titles than I have watches, almost.

Alexandra Willis: Superlative tennis writer. Works for Mr. Wimbledon. Once had to travel from Gare du Nord in Paris to the Roland Garros venue on the back of a motorbike. Please don't call her Alexander.

If you enjoyed this book I'd be very grateful if you leave a review. Thank you.

Printed in Great Britain
by Amazon.co.uk, Ltd.,
Marston Gate.